GW00722687

Red Hat OpenShift
Complete Self-Assessment Guid

The guidance in this Self-Assessment is b
practices and standards in business process architecture, design and
quality management. The guidance is also based on the professional
judgment of the individual collaborators listed in the Acknowledgments.

Notice of rights

Trademarks

Copyright © by The Art of Service
http://theartofservice.com
service@theartofservice.com

Table of Contents

About The Art of Service

The Art of Service, Business Process Architects since 2000, is dedicated to helping stakeholders achieve excellence.

Defining, designing, creating, and implementing a process to solve a stakeholders challenge or meet an objective is the most valuable role… In EVERY group, company, organization and department.

Unless you're talking a one-time, single-use project, there should be a process. Whether that process is managed and implemented by humans, AI, or a combination of the two, it needs to be designed by someone with a complex enough perspective to ask the right questions.

Someone capable of asking the right questions and step back and say, 'What are we really trying to accomplish here? And is there a different way to look at it?'

With The Art of Service's Standard Requirements Self-Assessments, we empower people who can do just that — whether their title is marketer, entrepreneur, manager, salesperson, consultant, Business Process Manager, executive assistant, IT Manager, CIO etc... —they are the people who rule the future. They are people who watch the process as it happens, and ask the right questions to make the process work better.

Contact us when you need any support with this Self-Assessment and any help with templates, blue-prints and examples of standard documents you might need:

http://theartofservice.com
service@theartofservice.com

Included Resources - how to access

Included with your purchase of the book is the Red Hat

OpenShift Self-Assessment Spreadsheet Dashboard which contains all questions and Self-Assessment areas and auto-generates insights, graphs, and project RACI planning - all with examples to get you started right away.

How? Simply send an email to **access@theartofservice.com** with this books' title in the subject to get the Red Hat OpenShift Self Assessment Tool right away.

You will receive the following contents with New and Updated specific criteria:

- The latest quick edition of the book in PDF

- The latest complete edition of the book in PDF, which criteria correspond to the criteria in...

- The Self-Assessment Excel Dashboard, and...

- Example pre-filled Self-Assessment Excel Dashboard to get familiar with results generation

- In-depth specific Checklists covering the topic

- Project management checklists and templates to assist with implementation

INCLUDES LIFETIME SELF ASSESSMENT UPDATES

Every self assessment comes with Lifetime Updates and Lifetime Free Updated Books. Lifetime Updates is an industry-first feature which allows you to receive verified self assessment updates, ensuring you always have the most accurate information at your fingertips.

Get it now- you will be glad you did - do it now, before you forget.

Send an email to **access@theartofservice.com** with this books' title in the subject to get the Red Hat OpenShift Self Assessment Tool right away.

Purpose of this Self-Assessment

This Self-Assessment has been developed to improve understanding of the requirements and elements of Red Hat OpenShift, based on best practices and standards in business process architecture, design and quality management.

It is designed to allow for a rapid Self-Assessment to determine how closely existing management practices and procedures correspond to the elements of the Self-Assessment.

The criteria of requirements and elements of Red Hat OpenShift have been rephrased in the format of a Self-Assessment questionnaire, with a seven-criterion scoring system, as explained in this document.

In this format, even with limited background knowledge of Red Hat OpenShift, a manager can quickly review existing operations to determine how they measure up to the standards. This in turn can serve as the starting point of a 'gap analysis' to identify management tools or system elements that might usefully be implemented in the organization to help improve overall performance.

How to use the Self-Assessment

On the following pages are a series of questions to identify to what extent your Red Hat OpenShift initiative is complete in comparison to the requirements set in standards.

To facilitate answering the questions, there is a space in front of each question to enter a score on a scale of '1' to '5'.

1 Strongly Disagree

2 Disagree

3 Neutral

4 Agree

5 Strongly Agree

Read the question and rate it with the following in front of mind:

'In my belief,
the answer to this question is clearly defined'.

There are two ways in which you can choose to interpret this statement;
1. how aware are you that the answer to the question is clearly defined
2. for more in-depth analysis you can choose to gather evidence and confirm the answer to the question. This obviously will take more time, most Self-Assessment users opt for the first way to interpret the question and dig deeper later on based on the outcome of the overall Self-Assessment.

A score of '1' would mean that the answer is not clear at all, where a '5' would mean the answer is crystal clear and defined. Leave emtpy when the question is not applicable or you don't want to answer it, you can skip it without affecting your score. Write your score in the space provided.

After you have responded to all the appropriate statements in each section, compute your average score for that section, using the formula provided, and round to the nearest tenth. Then transfer to the corresponding spoke in the Red Hat OpenShift Scorecard on the second next page of the Self-Assessment.

Your completed Red Hat OpenShift Scorecard will give you a clear presentation of which Red Hat OpenShift areas need attention.

Red Hat OpenShift
Scorecard Example

Example of how the finalized Scorecard can look like:

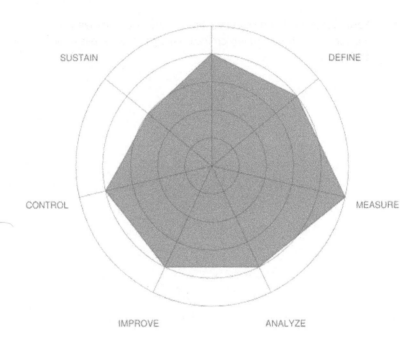

Red Hat OpenShift Scorecard

Your Scores:

BEGINNING OF THE SELF-ASSESSMENT:

CRITERION #1: RECOGNIZE

INTENT: Be aware of the need for change. Recognize that there is an unfavorable variation, problem or symptom.

In my belief, the answer to this question is clearly defined:

5 Strongly Agree

4 Agree

3 Neutral

2 Disagree

1 Strongly Disagree

1. What would happen if Red Hat OpenShift weren't done?
<--- Score

2. What is the biggest problem in Software Engineering?
<--- Score

3. What virtualization API is needed?

<--- Score

4. How much are sponsors, customers, partners, stakeholders involved in Red Hat OpenShift? In other words, what are the risks, if Red Hat OpenShift does not deliver successfully?
<--- Score

5. Why do you need container networking?
<--- Score

6. Why do you even need pods?
<--- Score

7. What are the stakeholder objectives to be achieved with Red Hat OpenShift?
<--- Score

8. What does Red Hat OpenShift success mean to the stakeholders?
<--- Score

9. How many applications does your environment need to support?
<--- Score

10. Why do you need yet another containers project like Kubernetes?
<--- Score

11. Is any extra configuration needed?
<--- Score

12. What do you need for running in a container?
<--- Score

13. What do you need to know to predict system properties from component properties?
<--- Score

14. Do you need to Authenticate?
<--- Score

15. Do you even need containers to be cloud native?
<--- Score

16. Who else hopes to benefit from it?
<--- Score

17. What is the hardest problem in Software Engineering?
<--- Score

18. What capabilities do you need?
<--- Score

19. Who needs a manager on a self-organizing team?
<--- Score

20. What do you need to pass into the container?
<--- Score

21. Which container port needs to be exposed?
<--- Score

22. When you use the docker run command, you need to consider how you want the container to run. For example, do you want it to run in the background and do its job, or do you need to interact with it?

<--- Score

23. Why would cookie-based persistence need to be used?
<--- Score

24. Do you need to create a local Docker Registry?
<--- Score

25. Microservices: how do you properly size services and identify boundaries?
<--- Score

26. How do you know how much you need?
<--- Score

27. Can the problem be fixed at the container level?
<--- Score

28. What is container orchestration and why do you need it?
<--- Score

29. If you do not specify what resources you need, what is OpenShifts default behavior?
<--- Score

30. What else do you need?
<--- Score

31. What are the problems faced due to containerization of goods?
<--- Score

32. How many replicas does your workload need?

<--- Score

33. Why do you need this?
<--- Score

34. As a sponsor, customer or management, how important is it to meet goals, objectives?
<--- Score

35. What do you need to be able to do this?
<--- Score

36. What problems does service mesh NOT solve?
<--- Score

37. How do you identify source of failures?
<--- Score

38. How many vms do you need?
<--- Score

39. What situation(s) led to this Red Hat OpenShift Self Assessment?
<--- Score

40. What systems need to be highly available?
<--- Score

41. What are the issues with virtual machines?
<--- Score

42. How are the Red Hat OpenShift's objectives aligned to the group's overall stakeholder strategy?
<--- Score

43. What problems are you facing and how do you

consider Red Hat OpenShift will circumvent those obstacles?
<--- Score

44. Does it offer integration with enterprise technologies to meet your needs today and in the future?
<--- Score

45. Are there any specific expectations or concerns about the Red Hat OpenShift team, Red Hat OpenShift itself?
<--- Score

46. Do you need to build an App for inventory management?
<--- Score

47. What do you need to change?
<--- Score

48. What are containers and why do you need them?
<--- Score

49. Do you need to go all in?
<--- Score

50. How are you going to measure success?
<--- Score

51. Do you need containers?
<--- Score

52. What are the expected benefits of Red Hat OpenShift to the stakeholder?

<--- Score

Add up total points for this section:
_____ = Total points for this section

Divided by: _____ (number of
statements answered) = _____
Average score for this section

Transfer your score to the Red Hat
OpenShift Index at the beginning of the
Self-Assessment.

CRITERION #2: DEFINE:

INTENT: Formulate the stakeholder problem. Define the problem, needs and objectives.

In my belief, the answer to this question is clearly defined:

5 Strongly Agree

4 Agree

3 Neutral

2 Disagree

1 Strongly Disagree

1. What are the rough order estimates on cost savings/ opportunities that Red Hat OpenShift brings?
<--- Score

2. Has the Red Hat OpenShift work been fairly and/ or equitably divided and delegated among team members who are qualified and capable to perform the work? Has everyone contributed?
<--- Score

3. When is the estimated completion date?
<--- Score

4. Can an application provide centralized network management to configure and manage multi-platform, Software defined, and traditional networking environment for academia and small business networks?
<--- Score

5. What critical content must be communicated – who, what, when, where, and how?
<--- Score

6. What services or functionality are required for a single workflow?
<--- Score

7. Is there a critical path to deliver Red Hat OpenShift results?
<--- Score

8. Has a project plan, Gantt chart, or similar been developed/completed?
<--- Score

9. Are there different segments of customers?
<--- Score

10. How will the Red Hat OpenShift team and the group measure complete success of Red Hat OpenShift?
<--- Score

11. Is the current 'as is' process being followed? If not,

what are the discrepancies?

<--- Score

12. How do you keep key subject matter experts in the loop?

<--- Score

13. Why does docker for windows require features required for virtualization?

<--- Score

14. When are meeting minutes sent out? Who is on the distribution list?

<--- Score

15. What are the key use cases for container-native virtualization?

<--- Score

16. Are stakeholder processes mapped?

<--- Score

17. Is a fully trained team formed, supported, and committed to work on the Red Hat OpenShift improvements?

<--- Score

18. Has anyone else (internal or external to the group) attempted to solve this problem or a similar one before? If so, what knowledge can be leveraged from these previous efforts?

<--- Score

19. What are the boundaries of the scope? What is in bounds and what is not? What is the start point? What is the stop point?

<--- Score

20. Are customer(s) identified and segmented according to their different needs and requirements?
<--- Score

21. What happens when none of services are appropriate for your use case?
<--- Score

22. Is Red Hat OpenShift currently on schedule according to the plan?
<--- Score

23. When is/was the Red Hat OpenShift start date?
<--- Score

24. What would be the goal or target for a Red Hat OpenShift's improvement team?
<--- Score

25. Do you find that the software in the package has sufficient functionality for your use case?
<--- Score

26. What does open mean in the context of building a hybrid cloud?
<--- Score

27. Roles: are the roles defined by the ip program correctly assigned?
<--- Score

28. Have the customer needs been translated into specific, measurable requirements? How?
<--- Score

29. How often are the team meetings?
<--- Score

30. Is there a failure scenario that would be common in the case of the storage system failing?
<--- Score

31. Will team members perform Red Hat OpenShift work when assigned and in a timely fashion?
<--- Score

32. Do the problem and goal statements meet the SMART criteria (specific, measurable, attainable, relevant, and time-bound)?
<--- Score

33. Has the improvement team collected the 'voice of the customer' (obtained feedback – qualitative and quantitative)?
<--- Score

34. What are the safety requirements for design?
<--- Score

35. How was the 'as is' process map developed, reviewed, verified and validated?
<--- Score

36. Are different versions of process maps needed to account for the different types of inputs?
<--- Score

37. Is data collected and displayed to better understand customer(s) critical needs and requirements.

<--- Score

38. Will team members regularly document their Red Hat OpenShift work?
<--- Score

39. Has a high-level 'as is' process map been completed, verified and validated?
<--- Score

40. How is the team tracking and documenting its work?
<--- Score

41. If substitutes have been appointed, have they been briefed on the Red Hat OpenShift goals and received regular communications as to the progress to date?
<--- Score

42. Given that there is no single, authoritative definition, when do you get to proclaim that your architecture is a microservice architecture?
<--- Score

43. Has the direction changed at all during the course of Red Hat OpenShift? If so, when did it change and why?
<--- Score

44. Are team charters developed?
<--- Score

45. What key stakeholder process output measure(s) does Red Hat OpenShift leverage and how?
<--- Score

46. What constraints exist that might impact the team?
<--- Score

47. Is the Red Hat OpenShift scope manageable?
<--- Score

48. Has/have the customer(s) been identified?
<--- Score

49. What specifically is the problem? Where does it occur? When does it occur? What is its extent?
<--- Score

50. Is Red Hat OpenShift linked to key stakeholder goals and objectives?
<--- Score

51. What do you do with a flow definition?
<--- Score

52. What are the Roles and Responsibilities for each team member and its leadership? Where is this documented?
<--- Score

53. Is the team sponsored by a champion or stakeholder leader?
<--- Score

54. Is full participation by members in regularly held team meetings guaranteed?
<--- Score

55. Is the team equipped with available and reliable

resources?
<--- Score

56. Who are the Red Hat OpenShift improvement team members, including Management Leads and Coaches?
<--- Score

57. How do containers redefine DevOps?
<--- Score

58. Is there a Red Hat OpenShift management charter, including stakeholder case, problem and goal statements, scope, milestones, roles and responsibilities, communication plan?
<--- Score

59. Has a team charter been developed and communicated?
<--- Score

60. Is the team formed and are team leaders (Coaches and Management Leads) assigned?
<--- Score

61. Is the team adequately staffed with the desired cross-functionality? If not, what additional resources are available to the team?
<--- Score

62. Are improvement team members fully trained on Red Hat OpenShift?
<--- Score

63. Has everyone on the team, including the team leaders, been properly trained?

<--- Score

64. Is there regularly 100% attendance at the team meetings? If not, have appointed substitutes attended to preserve cross-functionality and full representation?
<--- Score

65. How does the Red Hat OpenShift manager ensure against scope creep?
<--- Score

66. Is there a completed, verified, and validated high-level 'as is' (not 'should be' or 'could be') stakeholder process map?
<--- Score

67. What kinds of tools and technology are required for microservices?
<--- Score

68. What are the dynamics of the communication plan?
<--- Score

69. Does the team have regular meetings?
<--- Score

70. Are there any constraints known that bear on the ability to perform Red Hat OpenShift work? How is the team addressing them?
<--- Score

71. Is there a completed SIPOC representation, describing the Suppliers, Inputs, Process, Outputs, and Customers?

<--- Score

72. Are customers identified and high impact areas defined?
<--- Score

73. Do you make the guarantees required by the domain?
<--- Score

74. What policy research is required in this light?
<--- Score

75. How will variation in the actual durations of each activity be dealt with to ensure that the expected Red Hat OpenShift results are met?
<--- Score

76. What is your number-one use case for containers?
<--- Score

77. Is the improvement team aware of the different versions of a process: what they think it is vs. what it actually is vs. what it should be vs. what it could be?
<--- Score

78. What sorts of application integration with enterprise applications do you require?
<--- Score

79. What customer feedback methods were used to solicit their input?
<--- Score

80. What are the requirements for thinking about

containerization?

<--- Score

81. What are the compelling stakeholder reasons for embarking on Red Hat OpenShift?
<--- Score

82. How did the Red Hat OpenShift manager receive input to the development of a Red Hat OpenShift improvement plan and the estimated completion dates/times of each activity?
<--- Score

Add up total points for this section:
_ _ _ _ _ = Total points for this section

Divided by: _ _ _ _ _ _ (number of statements answered) = _ _ _ _ _ _
Average score for this section

Transfer your score to the Red Hat OpenShift Index at the beginning of the Self-Assessment.

CRITERION #3: MEASURE:

INTENT: Gather the correct data.
Measure the current performance and
evolution of the situation.

In my belief, the answer to this
question is clearly defined:

5 Strongly Agree

4 Agree

3 Neutral

2 Disagree

1 Strongly Disagree

1. Who participated in the data collection for measurements?
<--- Score

2. **What is the proposed new products financial potential, cost, and return on investment?**
<--- Score

3. **What will be the impact of accelerated**

speeds in your organization context and how can the transformational effects of cloud and containerization technologies be calibrated in a particular situation?
<--- Score

4. How do you measure lifecycle phases?
<--- Score

5. Have you found any 'ground fruit' or 'low-hanging fruit' for immediate remedies to the gap in performance?
<--- Score

6. How to root cause the issue when containers keep dying before you can access them?
<--- Score

7. Is Process Variation Displayed/Communicated?
<--- Score

8. What types of workloads is your organization prioritizing for containerization today?
<--- Score

9. Is from scratch the root of all docker images?
<--- Score

10. What makes root-cause analysis difficult?
<--- Score

11. Is data collected on key measures that were identified?
<--- Score

12. What has the team done to assure the stability and

accuracy of the measurement process?
<--- Score

13. How does the cloud impact and interface with the goals of IT Optimization?
<--- Score

14. What key measures identified indicate the performance of the stakeholder process?
<--- Score

15. Is data collection planned and executed?
<--- Score

16. How can the resource usage of a job running on a container-based cloud be measured?
<--- Score

17. What data was collected (past, present, future/ ongoing)?
<--- Score

18. What particular quality tools did the team find helpful in establishing measurements?
<--- Score

19. What are the agreed upon definitions of the high impact areas, defect(s), unit(s), and opportunities that will figure into the process capability metrics?
<--- Score

20. Will containerization cause your organization model break down?
<--- Score

21. Are high impact defects defined and identified in

the stakeholder process?
<--- Score

22. What do you do with root specifically?
<--- Score

23. Is there a Performance Baseline?
<--- Score

24. Are process variation components displayed/
communicated using suitable charts, graphs, plots?
<--- Score

25. What charts has the team used to display the
components of variation in the process?
<--- Score

26. Do you do big data analytics on-premises?
<--- Score

**27. What information do you use to do root-cause
analysis?**
<--- Score

28. Is a solid data collection plan established that
includes measurement systems analysis?
<--- Score

**29. How much does it cost for your system to go
down?**
<--- Score

30. Was a data collection plan established?
<--- Score

31. Will the new system be based on a full and true

cost analysis?
<--- Score

32. Are key measures identified and agreed upon?
<--- Score

33. How large is the gap between current performance and the customer-specified (goal) performance?
<--- Score

34. How do costs compare with continuing to use in-house facilities and systems?
<--- Score

35. Can power consumption and heat production be measured on container or pod level?
<--- Score

36. How exactly do you prioritize the migration of applications to the cloud?
<--- Score

37. Is long term and short term variability accounted for?
<--- Score

38. Is key measure data collection planned and executed, process variation displayed and communicated and performance baselined?
<--- Score

39. What are the key input variables? What are the key process variables? What are the key output variables?
<--- Score

40. Does the measured reliability of the system meet its specification?
<--- Score

41. Is that because of the nature of what service providers are doing, like in terms of just processing huge amounts of data all the time?
<--- Score

42. How do you use data and analytics to change the way fans experience the worlds largest annual sporting event?
<--- Score

Add up total points for this section:
_ _ _ _ _ = Total points for this section

Divided by: _ _ _ _ _ _ (number of statements answered) = _ _ _ _ _ _
Average score for this section

Transfer your score to the Red Hat OpenShift Index at the beginning of the Self-Assessment.

CRITERION #4: ANALYZE:

INTENT: Analyze causes, assumptions and hypotheses.

In my belief, the answer to this question is clearly defined:

5 Strongly Agree

4 Agree

3 Neutral

2 Disagree

1 Strongly Disagree

1. What were the financial benefits resulting from any 'ground fruit or low-hanging fruit' (quick fixes)?
<--- Score

2. Were Pareto charts (or similar) used to portray the 'heavy hitters' (or key sources of variation)?
<--- Score

3. Is the gap/opportunity displayed and communicated in financial terms?

<--- Score

4. How will the Red Hat OpenShift data be analyzed?

<--- Score

5. Does it require data persistence?

<--- Score

6. Did any value-added analysis or 'lean thinking' take place to identify some of the gaps shown on the 'as is' process map?

<--- Score

7. Was a cause-and-effect diagram used to explore the different types of causes (or sources of variation)?

<--- Score

8. What data should be provided, at what price (or free)?

<--- Score

9. How many samples/data points are needed?

<--- Score

10. Which stakeholder characteristics are analyzed?

<--- Score

11. Do corresponding spark/hadoop clusters need to share data sets?

<--- Score

12. What tools were used to generate the list of possible causes?

<--- Score

13. How do you white-list custom IP ranges to allow access to your Database service?
<--- Score

14. How beneficial would it be to bring all this data together?
<--- Score

15. Which secure transmission protocol is used to ensure the integrity of the logging data in transit?
<--- Score

16. Is there an option for you to make sure that your data is getting to you on the easiest, shortest, cleanest route?
<--- Score

17. What data do you make available on servers?
<--- Score

18. What drives container adoption?
<--- Score

19. What tools were used to narrow the list of possible causes?
<--- Score

20. Which data should be replicated?
<--- Score

21. How much information is enough for data quality information?
<--- Score

22. What are the systems/data that help

accomplish the process?
<--- Score

23. Is data and process analysis, root cause analysis and quantifying the gap/opportunity in place?
<--- Score

24. Are losses documented, analyzed, and remedial processes developed to prevent future losses?
<--- Score

25. Does your kubernetes solution equally support the private data center and public cloud endpoints that your business needs to deliver kubernetes on?
<--- Score

26. Why data in containers?
<--- Score

27. What security meta-data is available for your images?
<--- Score

28. What is your rollout process?
<--- Score

29. What kinds of practices and processes will you need to support microservices?
<--- Score

30. What restrictions does it impose on how you interact with your data?
<--- Score

31. What happens if your database application container dies?
<--- Score

32. How will the data be checked for quality?
<--- Score

33. Does Red Hat OpenShift systematically track and analyze outcomes for accountability and quality improvement?
<--- Score

34. Have all non-recommended alternatives been analyzed in sufficient detail?
<--- Score

35. Which technologies or trends will drive significant change or disruption?
<--- Score

36. What happens in data centre failure scenario ?
<--- Score

37. What does the data say about the performance of the stakeholder process?
<--- Score

38. How do you adopt a distributed development process?
<--- Score

39. Is all of your data in static files or will there be real-time data?
<--- Score

40. What controls are in place to prevent the

misuse of data by the already stated having access?

<--- Score

41. What if the whole datacenter goes dark?

<--- Score

42. Were there any improvement opportunities identified from the process analysis?

<--- Score

43. What are your key Red Hat OpenShift indicators that you will measure, analyze and track?

<--- Score

44. What databases are supported?

<--- Score

45. What are the ultimate consignee types and why is it required data field in the Automated Export System?

<--- Score

46. What conclusions were drawn from the team's data collection and analysis? How did the team reach these conclusions?

<--- Score

47. Have the types of risks that may impact Red Hat OpenShift been identified and analyzed?

<--- Score

48. Who most drives container adoption in your organization?

<--- Score

49. Do staff have the necessary skills to collect, analyze, and report data?

<--- Score

50. What are the revised rough estimates of the financial savings/opportunity for Red Hat OpenShift improvements?

<--- Score

51. Did any additional data need to be collected?

<--- Score

52. What part of your data needs persistency?

<--- Score

53. How can risk management be tied procedurally to process elements?

<--- Score

54. What quality tools were used to get through the analyze phase?

<--- Score

55. Why does a database need to provide data migration/ replication technology?

<--- Score

56. What were the crucial 'moments of truth' on the process map?

<--- Score

57. Does your organization systematically track and analyze outcomes related for accountability and quality improvement?

<--- Score

58. Is the Red Hat OpenShift process severely broken such that a re-design is necessary?
<--- Score

59. Have changes been properly/adequately analyzed for effect?
<--- Score

60. Have the problem and goal statements been updated to reflect the additional knowledge gained from the analyze phase?
<--- Score

61. What should be the role of your organization in providing data?
<--- Score

62. How to make it easy to find relevant profiling events in the profiling data?
<--- Score

63. Are pertinent alerts monitored, analyzed and distributed to appropriate personnel?
<--- Score

64. Is the performance gap determined?
<--- Score

65. Do you have a moral role as data scientist?
<--- Score

66. Were any designed experiments used to generate additional insight into the data analysis?
<--- Score

67. Are the conclusions adequately supported by the data shown?

<--- Score

68. Does your development to deployment process work effectively for your website team?

<--- Score

69. What is the cost of poor quality as supported by the team's analysis?

<--- Score

70. How was the detailed process map generated, verified, and validated?

<--- Score

71. How do you achieve the same level of automation in your data center, especially when you are running infrastructure products from more than one vendor?

<--- Score

72. How do you frame performance data to define and understand what success means for your marketing organization?

<--- Score

73. Can the cloud provider utilize any data stored on systems for any purpose outside organization use?

<--- Score

74. How do you keep data in storage when the container or pod is transient and nodes can fail?

<--- Score

75. Have any additional benefits been identified that will result from closing all or most of the gaps?
<--- Score

76. Are gaps between current performance and the goal performance identified?
<--- Score

77. Was a detailed process map created to amplify critical steps of the 'as is' stakeholder process?
<--- Score

78. Have the concerns of stakeholders to help identify and define potential barriers been obtained and analyzed?
<--- Score

79. Why does a database need to be cloud-agnostic or infrastructure-agnostic?
<--- Score

80. What are the data gravity characteristics of the application?
<--- Score

81. Which ai tools are used for data fusion & data assimilation?
<--- Score

82. What is the collaboration process like?
<--- Score

83. What did the team gain from developing a sub-process map?
<--- Score

84. How do you identify and analyze stakeholders and their interests?

<--- Score

85. What is offered as part of the Data Center choice enrollment?

<--- Score

Add up total points for this section:
_ _ _ _ _ = Total points for this section

Divided by: _ _ _ _ _ _ (number of statements answered) = _ _ _ _ _ _ Average score for this section

Transfer your score to the Red Hat OpenShift Index at the beginning of the Self-Assessment.

CRITERION #5: IMPROVE:

INTENT: Develop a practical solution. Innovate, establish and test the solution and to measure the results.

In my belief, the answer to this question is clearly defined:

5 Strongly Agree

4 Agree

3 Neutral

2 Disagree

1 Strongly Disagree

1. Is there a small-scale pilot for proposed improvement(s)? What conclusions were drawn from the outcomes of a pilot?
<--- Score

2. Is a contingency plan established?
<--- Score

3. Are the software developers responsive?

<--- Score

4. How do you improve Kubernetes networking?
<--- Score

5. Is pilot data collected and analyzed?
<--- Score

6. How will the team or the process owner(s) monitor the implementation plan to see that it is working as intended?
<--- Score

7. What are some typical use cases in which a developer or admin might want to use Docker?
<--- Score

8. How do you make it easy for developers to use it?
<--- Score

9. Are possible solutions generated and tested?
<--- Score

10. Are there common go-to solutions for the stakeholders or are there any mixtures of solutions utilized?
<--- Score

11. Is there a cost/benefit analysis of optimal solution(s)?
<--- Score

12. What alternative responses are available to manage risk?
<--- Score

13. How does the solution remove the key sources of issues discovered in the analyze phase?
<--- Score

14. What new functionality is required by either business objectives or development needs?
<--- Score

15. Are you are focused on cloud-native application development for new applications?
<--- Score

16. Can the anomaly detection quality be improved by incorporating event knowledge?
<--- Score

17. Can automated pull requests encourage software developers to upgrade out-of-date dependencies?
<--- Score

18. How do software engineers understand code changes?
<--- Score

19. What criteria will you use to assess your Red Hat OpenShift risks?
<--- Score

20. Why look at cloud optimization so soon after migrating?
<--- Score

21. Do you develop and test services locally, or within the cluster?

<--- Score

22. Is your development environment holding you back?
<--- Score

23. What technologies are your developers experts in?
<--- Score

24. Is the implementation plan designed?
<--- Score

25. Was a pilot designed for the proposed solution(s)?
<--- Score

26. How do application developers usually get corresponding features?
<--- Score

27. What is in the roadmap for autonomous operator?
<--- Score

28. What communications are necessary to support the implementation of the solution?
<--- Score

29. What is the result of all this for operations?
<--- Score

30. When developed a system what do you need to know from the components, from the systems and from the system usage?
<--- Score

31. Docker provides improvements for application virtualization, and what does it mean for security?
<--- Score

32. Do you want to develop and test services locally, or within the cluster?
<--- Score

33. How many open source developers does it take to change a light bulb?
<--- Score

34. How do you now get the values from this map into a pods container?
<--- Score

35. What error proofing will be done to address some of the discrepancies observed in the 'as is' process?
<--- Score

36. How does container-native virtualization differ from other Red Hat virtualization solutions?
<--- Score

37. When you develop a component what do you need to know about its usage in the future systems?
<--- Score

38. What tools were used to evaluate the potential solutions?
<--- Score

39. What does the 'should be' process map/design look like?
<--- Score

40. What do you optimize for?

<--- Score

41. How will the group know that the solution worked?

<--- Score

42. Which container infrastructure solution is right for you?

<--- Score

43. How can multi-modal point clouds be efficiently represented in a multi-resolution framework?

<--- Score

44. Describe the design of the pilot and what tests were conducted, if any?

<--- Score

45. What are the most common use cases for deployment of solutions?

<--- Score

46. Were any criteria developed to assist the team in testing and evaluating potential solutions?

<--- Score

47. What is it about the act of building a new container that improves reliability?

<--- Score

48. How, where, and why are containers leveraged in the software development life cycle?

<--- Score

49. Are you currently using or evaluating containers in your organization?
<--- Score

50. Is a solution implementation plan established, including schedule/work breakdown structure, resources, risk management plan, cost/budget, and control plan?
<--- Score

51. Which public cloud provider has the most developer-friendly environment for running containers?
<--- Score

52. What is Red Hat OpenShift's impact on utilizing the best solution(s)?
<--- Score

53. What does it take to actually implement microservice solutions?
<--- Score

54. What is the optimal size of a microservice?
<--- Score

55. How do you understand the enterprise requirements?
<--- Score

56. Are the best solutions selected?
<--- Score

57. Which specific solutions did fit Systems develop based on Red Hat technology?

<--- Score

58. How do you link measurement and risk?
<--- Score

59. Do you want to implement guide rails for your development teams?
<--- Score

60. What were the underlying assumptions on the cost-benefit analysis?
<--- Score

61. What if you could have your on-premises solution and your cloud solution, too?
<--- Score

62. Do you need instant solutions to your IT questions?
<--- Score

63. How did the team generate the list of possible solutions?
<--- Score

64. Is the optimal solution selected based on testing and analysis?
<--- Score

65. What tools were used to tap into the creativity and encourage 'outside the box' thinking?
<--- Score

66. How will you manage the life cycle of your Kubernetes solution?
<--- Score

67. What attendant changes will need to be made to ensure that the solution is successful?
<--- Score

68. What tools were most useful during the improve phase?
<--- Score

69. Do you know what companies are using services and have this risk?
<--- Score

70. Are new and improved process ('should be') maps developed?
<--- Score

71. What do you need to know to evaluate options for a cloud approach?
<--- Score

72. How do you present the results of a vulnerability scan of a Docker image in a format that is clear and detailed?
<--- Score

73. If you have a Kubernetes cluster, how can you leverage the capabilities to run your edge solution in an existing cluster?
<--- Score

74. How do you communicate with the developers?
<--- Score

75. How fast can tools be served to developers that need to become productive?

<--- Score

76. How do you develop and manage applications today?

<--- Score

77. What is the team's contingency plan for potential problems occurring in implementation?
<--- Score

78. What lessons, if any, from a pilot were incorporated into the design of the full-scale solution?
<--- Score

79. Are there any constraints (technical, political, cultural, or otherwise) that would inhibit certain solutions?
<--- Score

80. Can the anomaly detection quality be improved by incorporating architectural knowledge?

<--- Score

81. Do you really understand what the core structural abstractions are in your software?

<--- Score

82. What is the implementation plan?
<--- Score

83. Are improved process ('should be') maps modified based on pilot data and analysis?
<--- Score

Add up total points for this section:

_____ = Total points for this section

Divided by: _____ (number of
statements answered) = _____
Average score for this section

Transfer your score to the Red Hat
OpenShift Index at the beginning of the
Self-Assessment.

CRITERION #6: CONTROL:

INTENT: Implement the practical solution. Maintain the performance and correct possible complications.

In my belief, the answer to this question is clearly defined:

5 Strongly Agree

4 Agree

3 Neutral

2 Disagree

1 Strongly Disagree

1. Are operating procedures consistent?
<--- Score

2. Is new knowledge gained imbedded in the response plan?
<--- Score

3. What do you monitor?
<--- Score

4. What monitoring tools are you currently using?
<--- Score

5. What other systems, operations, processes, and infrastructures (hiring practices, staffing, training, incentives/rewards, metrics/dashboards/scorecards, etc.) need updates, additions, changes, or deletions in order to facilitate knowledge transfer and improvements?
<--- Score

6. How will input, process, and output variables be checked to detect for sub-optimal conditions?
<--- Score

7. When does your organization plan to make an investment in container technologies?
<--- Score

8. Is there any way that you can continue to pay for Docker Security Scanning Service in your Docker private repo plan?
<--- Score

9. Does a troubleshooting guide exist or is it needed?
<--- Score

10. Is there a standardized process?
<--- Score

11. Is admission control based on actual usage?
<--- Score

12. Is the service you are using adhering to open standards, or are you locked in?

<--- Score

13. How do you add security at scale and speed without impeding development?
<--- Score

14. What monitoring or management solutions are you using?
<--- Score

15. How are you monitoring 3rd party developer access?
<--- Score

16. Is admission control based on resource usage or resource request?
<--- Score

17. Does the platform monitor container availability, performance, and events?
<--- Score

18. Does the Red Hat OpenShift performance meet the customer's requirements?
<--- Score

19. Will any other parts of the Docker private repo plan change?
<--- Score

20. How do you monitor applications across clusters and clouds?
<--- Score

21. Who controls docker containers?
<--- Score

22. What are your plans for containerization systems, as Docker?

<--- Score

23. What is the control/monitoring plan?

<--- Score

24. What can containers bring to quality of service or scale of bandwidth?

<--- Score

25. Which other logging or tracing systems do you run alongside your monitoring tool?

<--- Score

26. Is the daemon set is the approach that you take when you have users that want to deploy monitoring across an entire Kubernetes cluster?

<--- Score

27. Is reporting being used or needed?

<--- Score

28. Are suggested corrective/restorative actions indicated on the response plan for known causes to problems that might surface?

<--- Score

29. Is there documentation that will support the successful operation of the improvement?

<--- Score

30. Will any special training be provided for results interpretation?

<--- Score

31. Are there documented procedures?
<--- Score

32. How might the group capture best practices and lessons learned so as to leverage improvements?
<--- Score

33. Have new or revised work instructions resulted?
<--- Score

34. Should you reject the request entirely, or should you alter it to meet your business standards?
<--- Score

35. What do you do if Docker for Planning Analytics Workspace hangs?
<--- Score

36. Does job training on the documented procedures need to be part of the process team's education and training?
<--- Score

37. Has the improved process and its steps been standardized?
<--- Score

38. What quality tools were useful in the control phase?
<--- Score

39. How do you manage & control team access to your clusters?
<--- Score

40. Why are the custom API server and the custom controller manager separate?

<--- Score

41. How will the process owner verify improvement in present and future sigma levels, process capabilities?

<--- Score

42. How do you monitor usage across clouds ?

<--- Score

43. How will the process owner and team be able to hold the gains?

<--- Score

44. Is knowledge gained on process shared and institutionalized?

<--- Score

45. How best to scale applications in the infrastructure to enable to work on corresponding data streams?

<--- Score

46. What is the clear-cut deployment plan?

<--- Score

47. How do you recover the standard docker volume data in the event of a host hardware failure?

<--- Score

48. Are you ready to scale?

<--- Score

49. What is the recommended frequency of auditing?
<--- Score

50. Is there a recommended audit plan for routine surveillance inspections of Red Hat OpenShift's gains?
<--- Score

51. What other areas of the group might benefit from the Red Hat OpenShift team's improvements, knowledge, and learning?
<--- Score

52. How to monitor services running on Kubernetes with Prometheus?
<--- Score

53. Is a response plan established and deployed?
<--- Score

54. Are documented procedures clear and easy to follow for the operators?
<--- Score

55. Is there a transfer of ownership and knowledge to process owner and process team tasked with the responsibilities.
<--- Score

56. How will new or emerging customer needs/ requirements be checked/communicated to orient the process toward meeting the new specifications and continually reducing variation?
<--- Score

57. Is there a documented and implemented monitoring plan?

<--- Score

58. How will the day-to-day responsibilities for monitoring and continual improvement be transferred from the improvement team to the process owner?
<--- Score

59. Does it scale in real life?
<--- Score

60. How do you monitor your Kubernetes cluster?
<--- Score

61. What should the next improvement project be that is related to Red Hat OpenShift?
<--- Score

62. How to monitor Kubernetes and containers with Prometheus?
<--- Score

63. Is there a control plan in place for sustaining improvements (short and long-term)?
<--- Score

64. Is the orchestration tool (implicitly) controlled by a single entity?
<--- Score

65. What key inputs and outputs are being measured on an ongoing basis?
<--- Score

66. Who is the Red Hat OpenShift process owner?
<--- Score

67. Are new process steps, standards, and documentation ingrained into normal operations?
<--- Score

68. Does the response plan contain a definite closed loop continual improvement scheme (e.g., plan-do-check-act)?
<--- Score

69. What are the critical parameters to watch?
<--- Score

70. Do you account for what a control plane is?
<--- Score

71. What is the effect on the replication controller?
<--- Score

72. How does fit Systems plan to leverage the Red Hat ecosystem in the future?
<--- Score

73. What kind of life-cycle environments do you plan to use (e.g., development, testing, staging, production)?
<--- Score

74. How will report readings be checked to effectively monitor performance?
<--- Score

75. What level of monitoring is provided?
<--- Score

76. How do you orchestrate/scale you Containers?

<--- Score

77. How does the solution scale?
<--- Score

78. How do you scale?
<--- Score

79. Is admission control based on resource usage or request?
<--- Score

80. Is a response plan in place for when the input, process, or output measures indicate an 'out-of-control' condition?
<--- Score

Add up total points for this section:
_ _ _ _ _ = Total points for this section

Divided by: _ _ _ _ _ _ (number of statements answered) = _ _ _ _ _ _
Average score for this section

Transfer your score to the Red Hat OpenShift Index at the beginning of the Self-Assessment.

CRITERION #7: SUSTAIN:

INTENT: Retain the benefits.

In my belief, the answer to this question is clearly defined:

5 Strongly Agree

4 Agree

3 Neutral

2 Disagree

1 Strongly Disagree

1. How does it compare to classic live migration or other approaches like Docker?
<--- Score

2. Production grade kubernetes: what does it mean?
<--- Score

3. Can you mix containers and hypervisors?
<--- Score

4. What challenges are you facing with your current storage infrastructure?
<--- Score

5. What is what an Azure container instance is behind the scenes?
<--- Score

6. Will what is inside the containers compromise your infrastructure?
<--- Score

7. What makes up a kubernetes cluster?
<--- Score

8. What are the challenges or differences between what service providers want and what enterprises want when it comes to private cloud?
<--- Score

9. What is the EA Workspace?
<--- Score

10. Are they configured only by the service provider?
<--- Score

11. How about your cluster and compute resources?
<--- Score

12. What packages do you use?
<--- Score

13. What benefits do container technologies offer your organization?

<--- Score

14. How do you do (agile) DevOps?
<--- Score

15. Why container orchestration?
<--- Score

16. What do you want to build?
<--- Score

17. What storage technology are you currently using?
<--- Score

18. Why is openshift secure when the underlying technologies are not?
<--- Score

19. How knowledgeable are you about what types of IT technologies your organization uses?
<--- Score

20. What is your scalability?
<--- Score

21. Who has access to What, When, How, and Why?
<--- Score

22. What is the relationship between products (as cloud foundry and openshift) and containers?
<--- Score

23. How do you deliver software value fast?
<--- Score

24. What if one of the already stated containers dies?

<--- Score

25. Why is this important?

<--- Score

26. Will the cloud change programming?

<--- Score

27. Which version of the technologies/Kubernetes is being offered?

<--- Score

28. What are the constraints for containerization of outbound packages?

<--- Score

29. How will you place containers near each other in your cluster?

<--- Score

30. What does this give your organization?

<--- Score

31. How to get to from one container on one host to a container on another?

<--- Score

32. Why are environment variables so popular in containers?

<--- Score

33. How do you design applications that can be easily moved from one cloud to another?

<--- Score

34. Why use vte with openshift?
<--- Score

35. Is your cluster working?
<--- Score

36. Do you have the bandwidth and skills to build your own platform from scratch?
<--- Score

37. Can containerization avoid becoming a victim of its own success?
<--- Score

38. When should you consider creating a bare-metal cluster?
<--- Score

39. Who are the container providers?
<--- Score

40. What happens if the Docker container has to be generated again?
<--- Score

41. Virtualization: what performs better?
<--- Score

42. How many different container orchestration tools do your organization use?
<--- Score

43. What are the security concerns with using containers?
<--- Score

44. Are organizations and systems negatively interdependent?

<--- Score

45. Where will enterprise content management go next?

<--- Score

46. What makes content effective?

<--- Score

47. How do you approach cloud migration?

<--- Score

48. What makes a flow Done?

<--- Score

49. What if you want to see what the environment is like inside the container?

<--- Score

50. Do you want the container to be highly available and if so, how?

<--- Score

51. What is docker-machine used for?

<--- Score

52. Can an existing enterprise distribution be streamlined?

<--- Score

53. How are you using Docker containers?

<--- Score

54. How do you keep your cluster up-to-date?
<--- Score

55. What are the primary reasons why you are replacing virtual machines with containers?
<--- Score

56. Are there new kinds of paradigms for securing your systems that are new to people who are used to having more of an imperative programming system?
<--- Score

57. Why application modernization ?
<--- Score

58. Will it work from host to host?
<--- Score

59. Have you considered how AI is changing the world around you already?
<--- Score

60. What is the security approach throughout the container life cycle?
<--- Score

61. How do you deploy this?
<--- Score

62. What is kubernetes missing?
<--- Score

63. What does a typical container-based architecture look like?
<--- Score

64. Which containers should be killed?
<--- Score

65. What does it mean to move an existing application to the cloud?
<--- Score

66. What version of OpenShift is that?
<--- Score

67. What are the key customer benefits of container-native virtualization?
<--- Score

68. Does your organization use application containerization in a production capacity today?
<--- Score

69. Have you got complex, realtime IoT applications?
<--- Score

70. How can aws help with scaling deployments?
<--- Score

71. What does effective patch management look like?
<--- Score

72. What is the primary reason why your organization is running container technologies?
<--- Score

73. Containers and the Enterprise, why now?
<--- Score

74. What principles did you build around?
<--- Score

75. Do services and apps interact appropriately?
<--- Score

76. What are the contenders ?
<--- Score

77. Where are your containers?
<--- Score

78. Are you close to hitting peak confusion regarding containers?
<--- Score

79. Why do you want to get started with containers?
<--- Score

80. Have you (or do you intend to) replace virtual machines with containers?
<--- Score

81. What is your current stage of Automation?
<--- Score

82. Why do you want this?
<--- Score

83. How do containers help your organization?
<--- Score

84. What resource limits should you put around the container?

<--- Score

85. What good is a container image if its only available on a single machine?
<--- Score

86. How do you really harvest the benefits of cloud services?
<--- Score

87. What is the knowledge stored in a repository of your organization?
<--- Score

88. What is your hybrid cloud strategy?
<--- Score

89. Why use linux containers?
<--- Score

90. How are services different from manufacturing?
<--- Score

91. What are the challenges?
<--- Score

92. How many application instances do you anticipate deploying in each OpenShift environment?
<--- Score

93. Why containers and not only Docker?
<--- Score

94. What if you want the pipeline to manage your

build and deployment based on a base image change?

<--- Score

95. What infrastructure will OpenShift run on?

<--- Score

96. Why would you want to self-host the ability to have a serverless architecture built on top of Kubernetes?

<--- Score

97. Are you considering or currently adopting Docker/Container technology?

<--- Score

98. Why should you treat stateful systems differently?

<--- Score

99. What are the gaps and pain points?

<--- Score

100. How to design reference architecture for visualizing enterprise knowledge?

<--- Score

101. Which public cloud providers do you currently use to run containers?

<--- Score

102. Is open source more secure than proprietary software?

<--- Score

103. How will you use docker-compose to display

the details of the running service?
<--- Score

104. If you use Kubernetes, how many production clusters do you have?
<--- Score

105. What if you run it on your infrastructure?
<--- Score

106. How much do your clients love you?
<--- Score

107. What happens when an open Docker server instance is found?
<--- Score

108. What is the topology of your network?
<--- Score

109. Do you get to a converged infrastructure?
<--- Score

110. Which services has service A access to?
<--- Score

111. What about operation systems compatibility?
<--- Score

112. How do you ensure load is evenly distributed across all containers?
<--- Score

113. Which departments should be involved?
<--- Score

114. What about the growth of the rack size?

<--- Score

115. What is the difference between Containers and Virtual Machines?

<--- Score

116. How does fit Systems leverage the Red Hat Partner Program?

<--- Score

117. Is it up-to-date?

<--- Score

118. Is it a software product you sell and want to deliver to your customers in containers?

<--- Score

119. What are other orchestrators?

<--- Score

120. Is open source the key to your IoT success?

<--- Score

121. What are you Integrating?

<--- Score

122. What is the maximum number of users?

<--- Score

123. What metrics should you use when?

<--- Score

124. How is a request to a service routed through Kubernetes?

<--- Score

125. What challenges do containers present to your organization?

<--- Score

126. How can a method for automating the extraction and vulnerability scanning of packages in a Docker image be constructed?

<--- Score

127. What will your organization gain?

<--- Score

128. How do you run N Kubernetes clusters as a service?

<--- Score

129. Is container-based technology a winner for your organizations high performance applications?

<--- Score

130. How is docker different from other container technologies?

<--- Score

131. What does change mean?

<--- Score

132. How to select hybrid cloud storage architectures?

<--- Score

133. Is the policy based on spreading load across resources?

<--- Score

134. Who owns what?
<--- Score

135. Will containers replace vms?
<--- Score

136. Who are your customers or users?
<--- Score

137. Which open source tools are helpful for your organization?
<--- Score

138. Do you rely on container technology and operate more than one Kubernetes cluster?
<--- Score

139. How is docker different from and disrupting traditional containers?
<--- Score

140. What do you want to achieve?
<--- Score

141. What are the other metrics that you are going to want to be looking at across your cluster?
<--- Score

142. Why have containers crossed the chasm?
<--- Score

143. How do you test many sessions?
<--- Score

144. What are your deployment strategies?

<--- Score

145. What is in your container stack?
<--- Score

146. What advantage does Kubernetes bring as a cluster manager?
<--- Score

147. Without openshift, is container image support for jboss eap / jws still important ?
<--- Score

148. How do you find the sweet spot for requests and limits?
<--- Score

149. What is your service mesh, exactly?
<--- Score

150. What does a service mesh actually do?
<--- Score

151. What is on your cluster?
<--- Score

152. Where will the java platform be deployed?
<--- Score

153. What types of distributions are being used?
<--- Score

154. Are you labelling your workloads properly?
<--- Score

155. What do you do with third-party-resources?

<--- Score

156. What if kubernetes can not be sure about your organization of the pod?
<--- Score

157. How do you move from keeping the lights on to driving innovation in the cloud?
<--- Score

158. How does docker handle security?
<--- Score

159. What if you want to update your code?
<--- Score

160. How strong and reliable are the isolation capabilities of Docker/Linux/OS containers?
<--- Score

161. How secure is it to host applications in Docker?
<--- Score

162. How can containers be made to utilize hardware-level separation features?
<--- Score

163. What happens when the pod dies?
<--- Score

164. Is holacracy succeeding at zappos?
<--- Score

165. Is the service mesh a networking model?
<--- Score

166. How will you schedule workloads most efficiently?

<--- Score

167. Which countries have open-source laws on the books?

<--- Score

168. Why do you want to containerize anything?

<--- Score

169. How long has your organization been making a financial investment in container technologies?

<--- Score

170. Is that the job of this kind of tooling that people plug into Kubernetes cluster?

<--- Score

171. How do you ship better (cloud) software faster?

<--- Score

172. What were the biggest roadblocks/challenges that you experienced when deploying container technology?

<--- Score

173. What happens if you crash?

<--- Score

174. Who really benefits from Open Source Clouds: users or providers?

<--- Score

175. How do customers experience the delivery of IT services?

<--- Score

176. Having understood what OpenShift is, what are the benefits of this Container platform?

<--- Score

177. What is in your App?

<--- Score

178. For which do you use containers today?

<--- Score

179. How does continuous integration fit into the cloud native journey?

<--- Score

180. What are the expected benefits of deploying container technologies at your organization?

<--- Score

181. Why openshift and not pure kubernetes?

<--- Score

182. Why are you reporting this research?

<--- Score

183. Does it have any known vulnerabilities?

<--- Score

184. Do you just give clients that cluster IP, maybe assign it a friendly domain name, and then add a route to get the already stated packets to one of the nodes?

<--- Score

185. How do you know that the Docker Host Integrity is there?

<--- Score

186. How do you place workloads based on capacity, policy?

<--- Score

187. Why would you want to use Microservices?

<--- Score

188. How do virtualized networks aid the separation of applications?

<--- Score

189. How do you handle edge deployments?

<--- Score

190. Is there any advantage to actually having Kubernetes running at the edge?

<--- Score

191. What happens if the node dies?

<--- Score

192. What are the future growth prospects of containerization?

<--- Score

193. Why do you want to invest in containers?

<--- Score

194. Is your organization making a financial investment in container technologies?

<--- Score

195. How secure is it to host applications with container techniques as Docker?

<--- Score

196. What is your service mesh?

<--- Score

197. How do containers communicate with one another, and what happens if a given container fails and becomes unresponsive?

<--- Score

198. How to stop and restart the Docker container?

<--- Score

199. What is it about containers that makes them so widely popular?

<--- Score

200. Are you ready for SDN?

<--- Score

201. If you use OpenShift does this mean all of your environments will be in the same place, as this sounds dangerous?

<--- Score

202. What does a scheduler actually do?

<--- Score

203. How can corresponding cloud services be tested for performance?

<--- Score

204. What is the advantage of the Chromebook

security model?
<--- Score

205. Is this kubernetes cluster secure?
<--- Score

206. Why are technologies seeing so much momentum right now?
<--- Score

207. What if it is very slow?
<--- Score

208. How is kubernetes a useful tool for running software at the edge?
<--- Score

209. Will your organization provide source or content?
<--- Score

210. Who are your users and how are you interacting with them?
<--- Score

211. With your pod running, how do you access it?
<--- Score

212. What should you test?
<--- Score

213. When you store information in a public cloud, do you get it back out?
<--- Score

214. Why is openshift the best platform?

<--- Score

215. Can kubernetes reach the container registry and actually pull the container image?
<--- Score

216. How frequently will the container be updated and how will you know when its updated?
<--- Score

217. What do you think will be the next open source tech trends?
<--- Score

218. Bake server images (AMIs) or use containers?
<--- Score

219. Where might cloud-native applications appear?
<--- Score

220. Managed by a cloud provider or you want to manage?
<--- Score

221. Can it run on a public cloud provider?
<--- Score

222. Is the docker daemon running on this host?
<--- Score

223. How secure is your container pipeline?
<--- Score

224. What is your primary source for container platform technologies?

<--- Score

225. Which container should be killed?
<--- Score

226. What level of interface abstraction is appropriate for the automation tooling?
<--- Score

227. What is supported on OpenShift ?
<--- Score

228. Do you have to be a startup jockey to get something out of corresponding sessions?
<--- Score

229. What is the hard part?
<--- Score

230. Why did you go to containerization?
<--- Score

231. Are you working today with any of container technologies?
<--- Score

232. Did you restrict the containers resource usage?
<--- Score

233. Is the platform Multi-tenant?
<--- Score

234. Why red hat openshift for public sector?
<--- Score

235. Are all services running as expected?
<--- Score

236. Are software images kept in a private registry?
<--- Score

237. Why do customers care about Containers?
<--- Score

238. Who are the target customers, users, and buyers?
<--- Score

239. Is your organization an established enterprise?
<--- Score

240. Is docker offering a safe environment to run applications?
<--- Score

241. Is your application fast?
<--- Score

242. What are the smart policies?
<--- Score

243. Where does your research advance your knowledge of the fundamental laws governing time and matter?
<--- Score

244. What does the release manager do?
<--- Score

245. What are the benefits of patch management?
<--- Score

246. How do you get your code into the cluster in a repeatable, reliable way?
<--- Score

247. Is running spark jobs on kubernetes a good idea?
<--- Score

248. What is the Cloud Native mindset?
<--- Score

249. What would a block storage capability offer if purpose-built for container-based cloud platforms?
<--- Score

250. When to opt for containers as a service?
<--- Score

251. What is container orchestration?
<--- Score

252. How do you specify the configuration ?
<--- Score

253. How is the network connectivity?
<--- Score

254. Is that something that you could definitely have to deal with in a couple of years?
<--- Score

255. How important are benefits of containers to

your organization?

<--- Score

256. How can multi-modal point clouds be efficiently displayed on emerging display technologies?

<--- Score

257. Why choose containers?

<--- Score

258. What are your current team or group divisions?

<--- Score

259. What is docker (aside from more awesomeness)?

<--- Score

260. What type of platform will you deploy containers on?

<--- Score

261. How much time does it take to provision a cluster?

<--- Score

262. How does the container know how to connect to all corresponding different storage types?

<--- Score

263. What logging tools are you currently using?

<--- Score

264. When a user establishes a watch connection to the API server by adding the query parameter ?

<--- Score

265. Does your organization currently use container technologies?
<--- Score

266. How have your customers gone hybrid with OpenShift?
<--- Score

267. Why are docker images lightweight?
<--- Score

268. What are the primary threats to container environments?
<--- Score

269. What can container orchestration tools do?
<--- Score

270. What else do you do within the default Docker steps?
<--- Score

271. What types of traffic are allowed to flow between the already stated services?
<--- Score

272. Are there known vulnerabilities in the application layer?
<--- Score

273. What network plugin providers are you using?
<--- Score

274. Are there any upcoming challenges to the API infrastructure that you are seeing on the horizon?

<--- Score

275. What is involved in managing containers?

<--- Score

276. What does it affect?

<--- Score

277. Are any privileged Docker containers allowed?

<--- Score

278. What is edge for you?

<--- Score

279. How can you get a Docker container ?

<--- Score

280. What are the types of supporting technologies you built for this change in environment?

<--- Score

281. How much memory are the workers using?

<--- Score

282. Did the services session affinity change in the meantime?

<--- Score

283. What does it take to achieve production-quality, well-supported open source software?

<--- Score

284. Which framework offers greater support for aggregation and personalization of user preferences?

<--- Score

285. How does container-native virtualization enhance OpenShift Container Platform?

<--- Score

286. Who manages the system it runs on?

<--- Score

287. Why converged infrastructure?

<--- Score

288. Who is going to mentor newcomers in open source projects?

<--- Score

289. What is your Kubernetes upgrade strategy?

<--- Score

290. How do you use DNS to do service discovery in Kubernetes?

<--- Score

291. What is your patch management?

<--- Score

292. Does docker support multiple architectures?

<--- Score

293. Who wrote the container image?

<--- Score

294. What do you mean by containerization?

<--- Score

295. Why would technological enthusiasts want to make use of Docker?

<--- Score

296. What about virtualization/ containerization?

<--- Score

297. How do you architect your Kubernetes cluster?

<--- Score

298. How is openshift container platform secured?

<--- Score

299. What makes this complex?

<--- Score

300. Which public cloud provider do you view as the best value for money?

<--- Score

301. What are your challenges in using/deploying containers?

<--- Score

302. How is the team organized?

<--- Score

303. Analog: what size VM should you use?

<--- Score

304. What would you change?

<--- Score

305. What is a container and how are containers used?
<--- Score

306. What has docker done for your organization?
<--- Score

307. What do you want to run on it?
<--- Score

308. Do you want to use the resource pool created on the host or cluster?
<--- Score

309. How do containers help transform it?
<--- Score

310. What is a pattern for a distributed system?
<--- Score

311. Where are you headed?
<--- Score

312. When to opt for custom deployment?
<--- Score

313. How to handle containers deployment to the edge?
<--- Score

314. How can container-based storage be implemented?
<--- Score

315. Who is responsible for what?
<--- Score

316. Do you have access to configuration history?
<--- Score

317. What is the best deployment approach?
<--- Score

318. What do you want to test?
<--- Score

319. What are you exploring using AI for?
<--- Score

320. What are the challenges of hardening?
<--- Score

321. Why openshift on openstack?
<--- Score

322. What happens when a container/machine disappears?
<--- Score

323. How will you use docker-compose to run an application in daemon mode?
<--- Score

324. How did the introduction of the smartphone changed the API topology?
<--- Score

325. How does container-native virtualization work?
<--- Score

326. Is there anything that strikes you as odd?

<--- Score

327. What happens if a host has trouble?
<--- Score

328. What does it mean to be Production Grade ?
<--- Score

329. How do you manage API Gateway topology?
<--- Score

330. How kubernetes differs from docker project?
<--- Score

331. How aggressively did you start throwing services on to it?
<--- Score

332. Can a software supply chain be completely secure?
<--- Score

333. Is your organization running container technologies in production?
<--- Score

334. What about existing workloads?
<--- Score

335. How can corresponding Containers be deployed in a reliable and reproducible manner?
<--- Score

336. Which command included in Kubernetes is the main tool that is used to deploy and manage applications on a Kubernetes cluster?

<--- Score

337. Which metrics are relevant?
<--- Score

338. Do you securely store and manage your Docker images?
<--- Score

339. Who are the major players in the container runtime space?
<--- Score

340. How do you test your code?
<--- Score

341. How many public images are there on docker hub?
<--- Score

342. Is your organization using serverless technology?
<--- Score

343. How will you move containers between different nodes on your cluster?
<--- Score

344. When is openshift a good fit?
<--- Score

345. What files make up a virtual machine?
<--- Score

346. Do containers have anything to do with that?
<--- Score

347. What are the formats of the knowledge stored?

<--- Score

348. What can be displayed in the GIS-based visualization interface?

<--- Score

349. Why do it this way?

<--- Score

350. How will you determine the exact version of the Linux kernel and of Docker running on your system?

<--- Score

351. Do you still benefit from the cloud?

<--- Score

352. How do you get containers to be production ready?

<--- Score

353. How will you automatically recover when a container fails?

<--- Score

354. What are containers and kubernetes?

<--- Score

355. Will a virtualization-centric strategy in the age of containerization represent an opportunity loss or remain at the core of unmet business demands?

<--- Score

356. Who is fit Systems, and what does it offer?
<--- Score

357. Is the container that you rolled out here, is it going to conflict on a port level?
<--- Score

358. How do you back up your applications?
<--- Score

359. How do you make Kubernetes Networking fast, flexible, and scalable?
<--- Score

360. Does the vendor respond to bugs and feature requests, even from smaller customers?
<--- Score

361. How could the integration be better?
<--- Score

362. What happens when you deploy virtualized network services inside Docker?
<--- Score

363. How can wiki support presentation of enterprise knowledge?
<--- Score

364. Microservices: why should you care?
<--- Score

365. What release are you currently running?
<--- Score

366. What role does a service mesh play in your security policy?

<--- Score

367. How skilled is your team in the use of containers?

<--- Score

368. What is your approach to integrating the latest technologies available in the ever-evolving cloud toolkit?

<--- Score

369. Which type of VM should you use?

<--- Score

370. Do you think that well see changes like that in the way that people purchase and deploy software?

<--- Score

371. How do you set up API Manager metrics?

<--- Score

372. Why would you want to create your own?

<--- Score

373. What kubernetes ingress providers are you using?

<--- Score

374. Can they do any real damage?

<--- Score

375. What are your microservices?

<--- Score

376. What is the difference between Docker and other container technologies?

<--- Score

377. Which services can access service A?

<--- Score

378. Do teams have conflicting goals?

<--- Score

379. How do you run Kubernetes?

<--- Score

380. How do you schedule workloads most efficiently?

<--- Score

381. How much of your organizations containers are built and run in IT environments?

<--- Score

382. What about high availability?

<--- Score

383. What was the strategic reason fit Systems selected Red Hat as a partner?

<--- Score

384. How does red hat and openshift manage security?

<--- Score

385. What if the service is a web server and users must access it from outside the cluster?

<--- Score

386. Why is docker security scanning being removed as an option?
<--- Score

387. How do you get to the staging environment?
<--- Score

388. Which container orchestration tools does your organization use?
<--- Score

389. What happens when a pod crashes?
<--- Score

390. What is your success/fail ratio?
<--- Score

391. What business capabilities does this affect?
<--- Score

392. Can ai be used as forward operator?
<--- Score

393. Where are you on your cloud journey?
<--- Score

394. Where do your containers come from?
<--- Score

395. What type of knowledge is stored?
<--- Score

396. How do you decide which products to direct resources towards?
<--- Score

397. How about services with a label named component?

<--- Score

398. Should user-centric design be integrated into the network hierarchy and where?

<--- Score

399. Which vendors have the most to gain from the adoption of containers?

<--- Score

400. How stable is the interface between kernel versions or operating systems?

<--- Score

401. How knowledgeable are you about how much money is invested in IT technologies your organization uses?

<--- Score

402. Do containers enhance security on its own?

<--- Score

403. What version of Kubernetes does your organization support?

<--- Score

404. How fast you can introduce a new framework into your cloud?

<--- Score

405. Are there any security anti-patterns that you see commonly executed with people deploying kubernetes infrastructure?

<--- Score

406. What kind of information would you like to see or receive?
<--- Score

407. Do you break the load into smaller parts?
<--- Score

408. Do you isolate pieces in separate containers without massive rewrite?
<--- Score

409. What are you writing code with?
<--- Score

410. How else do containers change enterprise security?
<--- Score

411. Are you interested in learning more about the advantages of running Docker on the mainframe?
<--- Score

412. How do you ensure container security and compliance?
<--- Score

413. How do you assess your security posture?
<--- Score

414. Did containers live up to the hype?
<--- Score

415. What fits your application best?
<--- Score

416. Are you a cloud native or just a cloud migrant?

<--- Score

417. How are you going to change your application to suit containers?

<--- Score

418. How should the App behave when it receives a termination signal?

<--- Score

419. What if, for whatever reason, you can not access your service?

<--- Score

420. What are the main differences between the systems when running containers in cloud environments?

<--- Score

421. What do you want in out of every service in terms of security?

<--- Score

422. Are you sure there is not a better way?

<--- Score

423. Where are your services running?

<--- Score

424. Do you want to participate and contribute as well, or rely on your vendor to curate and enhance the best open source components for you?

<--- Score

425. Who are the most successful open-source based companies?
<--- Score

426. Do you have an opinion on code repository structure?
<--- Score

427. What does container-native virtualization do?
<--- Score

428. Which orchestration tool did you choose?
<--- Score

429. What is a knowledge worker and a peak concurrent agent?
<--- Score

430. What public cloud provider do you view as the best value for the money?
<--- Score

431. Why is it important to build cloud native applications?
<--- Score

432. What version do you pick?
<--- Score

433. What about docker swarm?
<--- Score

434. Why stateful containers?
<--- Score

435. Why is docker security important?
<--- Score

436. What does your application do?
<--- Score

437. Who will operate containers?
<--- Score

438. What storage challenges have you experienced when trying to run stateful containers?
<--- Score

439. Does the docker implementation enable encryption of its images?
<--- Score

440. Can there be edge operators as a business model?
<--- Score

441. Does the platform provide a private image registry?
<--- Score

442. How do you manage clusters as if they were one environment ?
<--- Score

443. What are the software subscription license components?
<--- Score

444. What were the pros and cons to building your organization around an open source project?

<--- Score

445. Why a container management platform?
<--- Score

446. What kind of traffic do you expect?
<--- Score

447. What is new in the UML space?
<--- Score

448. Is this approach mature and enterprise ready?
<--- Score

449. Are your vendors network topologies aligned?
<--- Score

450. Which of corresponding cloud native storage projects is your organization using?
<--- Score

451. Will ignoring containerization as an encapsulation strategy lead to a competitive disadvantage?
<--- Score

452. Why did you adopt containers in addition to PaaS?
<--- Score

453. When will container-native virtualization be available?
<--- Score

454. How comfortable (and capable) is the team in

regard to automation?

<--- Score

455. How does docker change security landscape?

<--- Score

456. What if the node fails exactly when the App tries to do that?

<--- Score

457. Are container techniques as Docker suitable for deploying applications to the cloud?

<--- Score

458. How do you set consistent security policies across environments ?

<--- Score

459. What makes a container cluster?

<--- Score

460. How many containers does your organization typically run?

<--- Score

461. How is wiki supporting enterprise knowledge visualization?

<--- Score

462. What percentage of your apps are running in containers?

<--- Score

463. Does your organization run container technologies?

<--- Score

464. How can aws help with operational complexity?

<--- Score

465. How do you install and start with Docker ?

<--- Score

466. What practical steps can organizations take to reasonably secure containers?

<--- Score

467. What happens when you remove containers with volumes?

<--- Score

468. Is your installation supported if integrating with other Red Hat technologies?

<--- Score

469. Do you trust the security of your networks and firewalls?

<--- Score

470. Is there a limit on the size of your Docker image?

<--- Score

471. Where does docker fit in the DevOps puzzle?

<--- Score

472. How will container-native virtualization be made available?

<--- Score

473. What are the possible pitfalls to

containerization?

<--- Score

474. How do you specify the configuration?

<--- Score

475. Is it possible to limit resources in a container?

<--- Score

476. Why nobody contributes to your super open source project?

<--- Score

477. Which public cloud provider do you view as most reliable for running containers?

<--- Score

478. What is the challenge?

<--- Score

479. What is the big deal about containers?

<--- Score

480. How do you design a program repair bot?

<--- Score

481. What makes an application Cloud Native?

<--- Score

482. What if kubernetes itself fails?

<--- Score

483. What is the right way to deploy containers successfully?

<--- Score

484. Are there limitations to using docker?
<--- Score

485. How do source code reviews of security products work?
<--- Score

486. Should the pod remain the unit of work for a cluster federation?
<--- Score

487. How does docker differ from a virtual machine?
<--- Score

488. Why have a separate custom API server?
<--- Score

489. How do docker containers communicate across nodes?
<--- Score

490. What is the existing framework within your organization?
<--- Score

491. How to get to the already stated containers from outside?
<--- Score

492. How can the application be shielded?
<--- Score

493. What container configuration file formats and runtime environments are supported?
<--- Score

494. How would you deploy that in terms of Docker containers?

<--- Score

495. Are you familiar with Serverless Functions and Docker containers ?

<--- Score

496. What exactly is your sandbox?

<--- Score

497. What does it mean to create applications in a truly cloud-native manner?

<--- Score

498. What are the difficulties in setting up your own Kubernetes cluster?

<--- Score

499. What is the difference between docker run and docker create?

<--- Score

500. How can aws help with managing apis?

<--- Score

501. Which framework fits both in the short-term and long-term IT and business strategy of your organization?

<--- Score

502. What is your container orchestration?

<--- Score

503. Will docker replace virtual machines?

<--- Score

504. Have containers made your job easier or harder?
<--- Score

505. Which platforms have the most to lose from adoption of containers?
<--- Score

506. How much platform should you build?
<--- Score

507. How do you use Containers safely?
<--- Score

508. What is the Container Network Interface?
<--- Score

509. What, exactly, is a container, and what does Docker have to do with it?
<--- Score

510. What do you see in the container logs?
<--- Score

511. What should service discovery provide?
<--- Score

512. What about other container orchestration tools?
<--- Score

513. How many containers is your organization running in production?
<--- Score

514. Why containerize applications?

<--- Score

515. What top benefits are the already stated using containers seeing today?

<--- Score

516. What about stateful apps?

<--- Score

517. How do you move workloads across corresponding environments?

<--- Score

518. How does openshift help you take advantage of linux containers?

<--- Score

519. What about restores?

<--- Score

520. How much of an annual financial investment has your organization made in personnel expenses to use container technologies?

<--- Score

521. How is wiki supporting presentation of enterprise knowledge?

<--- Score

522. Is the status of each virtual machine up?

<--- Score

523. What kind of cloud services can and should be used to host scalable IoT applications?

<--- Score

524. What if your application is composed of multiple containers?
<--- Score

525. Are docker containers really secure?
<--- Score

526. Is it important for your organization to secure devices through containerization?
<--- Score

527. Best free open source alternatives to Windows 10: what is the best open source OS?
<--- Score

528. What applications are running within containers?
<--- Score

529. Can run enterprise apps in a single docker container?
<--- Score

530. Does the container run standalone, locally (that is, outside of Kubernetes)?
<--- Score

531. Why should you run a single cluster for multiple isolated users or deployments?
<--- Score

532. How do you manage cloud services (as PaaS and SaaS)?
<--- Score

533. Why composite application support?

<--- Score

534. What does kubernetes not cover ?

<--- Score

535. How do you operate apps and services on and around Kubernetes?

<--- Score

536. Which container orchestration tools does your organization use / use most frequently?

<--- Score

537. What is the difference between a virtual machine and a container?

<--- Score

538. How do you deploy and manage all of running containers?

<--- Score

Add up total points for this section:
_ _ _ _ _ = Total points for this section

Divided by: _ _ _ _ _ _ (number of
statements answered) = _ _ _ _ _ _
Average score for this section

Transfer your score to the Red Hat
OpenShift Index at the beginning of the
Self-Assessment.

Red Hat OpenShift and Managing Projects, Criteria for Project Managers:

1.0 Initiating Process Group: Red Hat OpenShift

1. Were resources available as planned?

2. Establishment of pm office?

3. Did the Red Hat OpenShift project team have the right skills?

4. When will the Red Hat OpenShift project be done?

5. At which stage, in a typical Red Hat OpenShift project do stake holders have maximum influence?

6. What communication items need improvement?

7. Were decisions made in a timely manner?

8. Professionals want to know what is expected from them what are the deliverables?

9. Contingency planning. if a risk event occurs, what will you do?

10. How well did you do?

11. What is the stake of others in your Red Hat OpenShift project?

12. When are the deliverables to be generated in each phase?

13. During which stage of Risk planning are risks prioritized based on probability and impact?

14. Realistic - are the desired results expressed in a way that the team will be motivated and believe that the required level of involvement will be obtained?

15. Will the Red Hat OpenShift project meet the client requirements, and will it achieve the business success criteria that justified doing the Red Hat OpenShift project in the first place?

16. The Red Hat OpenShift project you are managing has nine stakeholders. How many channel of communications are there between corresponding stakeholders?

17. How will you do it?

18. Are the Red Hat OpenShift project team and stakeholders meeting regularly and using a meeting agenda and taking notes to accurately document what is being covered and what happened in the weekly meetings?

19. Did the Red Hat OpenShift project team have the right skills?

20. For technology Red Hat OpenShift projects only: Are all production support stakeholders (Business unit, technical support, & user) prepared for implementation with appropriate contingency plans?

1.1 Project Charter: Red Hat OpenShift

21. Are you building in-house ?

22. Avoid costs, improve service, and/ or comply with a mandate?

23. Must Have?

24. How do you manage integration?

25. Who will take notes, document decisions?

26. Why have you chosen the aim you have set forth?

27. Why use a Red Hat OpenShift project charter?

28. Will this replace an existing product?

29. What material?

30. What are the assumptions?

31. What goes into your Red Hat OpenShift project Charter?

32. For whom?

33. How will you know that a change is an improvement?

34. Who is the sponsor?

35. Customer: who are you doing the Red Hat OpenShift project for?

36. Red Hat OpenShift project background: what is the primary motivation for this Red Hat OpenShift project?

37. Strategic fit: what is the strategic initiative identifier for this Red Hat OpenShift project?

38. What is the justification?

39. Why do you manage integration?

40. When is a charter needed?

1.2 Stakeholder Register: Red Hat OpenShift

41. How much influence do they have on the Red Hat OpenShift project?

42. What is the power of the stakeholder?

43. Is your organization ready for change?

44. How should employers make voices heard?

45. Who wants to talk about Security?

46. What are the major Red Hat OpenShift project milestones requiring communications or providing communications opportunities?

47. What & Why?

48. How will reports be created?

49. What opportunities exist to provide communications?

50. Who are the stakeholders?

51. Who is managing stakeholder engagement?

52. How big is the gap?

1.3 Stakeholder Analysis Matrix: Red Hat OpenShift

53. Why do you need to manage Red Hat OpenShift project Risk?

54. Cashflow, start-up cash-drain?

55. Who will be affected by the work?

56. Which conditions out of the control of the management are crucial for the achievement of the immediate objective?

57. Accreditations, etc?

58. Who is most dependent on the resources at stake?

59. Legislative effects?

60. Accreditations, qualifications, certifications?

61. How to measure the achievement of the Development Objective?

62. How affected by the problem(s)?

63. Where are mitigation costs factored in?

64. Sustaining internal capabilities?

65. Disadvantages of proposition?

66. What tools would help you communicate?

67. Are there two or three that rise to the top, and a couple that are sliding to the bottom?

68. Are the required specifications for products or services changing?

69. What is the relationship among stakeholders?

70. Could any of your organizations weaknesses seriously threaten development?

71. What is your Advocacy Strategy?

72. How do customers express needs?

2.0 Planning Process Group: Red Hat OpenShift

73. If a task is partitionable, is this a sufficient condition to reduce the Red Hat OpenShift project duration?

74. The Red Hat OpenShift project charter is created in which Red Hat OpenShift project management process group?

75. What do you need to do?

76. Just how important is your work to the overall success of the Red Hat OpenShift project?

77. Red Hat OpenShift project assessment; why did you do this Red Hat OpenShift project?

78. What will you do?

79. If action is called for, what form should it take?

80. How should needs be met?

81. Professionals want to know what is expected from them; what are the deliverables?

82. Does it make any difference if you are successful?

83. How does activity resource estimation affect activity duration estimation?

84. How well will the chosen processes produce the expected results?

85. To what extent has the intervention strategy been adapted to the areas of intervention in which it is being implemented?

86. On which process should team members spend the most time?

87. Is the schedule for the set products being met?

88. Is the Red Hat OpenShift project supported by national and/or local organizations?

89. Does the program have follow-up mechanisms (to verify the quality of the products, punctuality of delivery, etc.) to measure progress in the achievement of the envisaged results?

90. To what extent are the participating departments coordinating with each other?

91. To what extent is the program helping to influence your organizations policy framework?

2.1 Project Management Plan: Red Hat OpenShift

92. If the Red Hat OpenShift project is complex or scope is specialized, do you have appropriate and/or qualified staff available to perform the tasks?

93. Are there any scope changes proposed for a previously authorized Red Hat OpenShift project?

94. Is the appropriate plan selected based on your organizations objectives and evaluation criteria expressed in Principles and Guidelines policies?

95. Development trends and opportunities. What if the positive direction and vision of your organization causes expected trends to change?

96. Who is the Red Hat OpenShift project Manager?

97. How well are you able to manage your risk?

98. What is Red Hat OpenShift project scope management?

99. Are there any Client staffing expectations?

100. What would you do differently what did not work?

101. Was the peer (technical) review of the cost estimates duly coordinated with the cost estimate center of expertise and addressed in the review

documentation and certification?

102. How do you organize the costs in the Red Hat OpenShift project management plan?

103. When is a Red Hat OpenShift project management plan created?

104. Do the proposed changes from the Red Hat OpenShift project include any significant risks to safety?

105. How do you manage time?

106. Are the existing and future without-plan conditions reasonable and appropriate?

107. Are the proposed Red Hat OpenShift project purposes different than a previously authorized Red Hat OpenShift project?

108. What should you drop in order to add something new?

109. What is the business need?

2.2 Scope Management Plan: Red Hat OpenShift

110. Are there checklists created to demine if all quality processes are followed?

111. Is pert / critical path or equivalent methodology being used?

112. The greatest degree of uncertainty is encountered during which phase of the Red Hat OpenShift project life cycle?

113. Is there an onboarding process in place?

114. Are corrective actions taken when actual results are substantially different from detailed Red Hat OpenShift project plan (variances)?

115. Has the Red Hat OpenShift project manager been identified?

116. What do you need to do to accomplish the goal or goals?

117. What went wrong?

118. Are actuals compared against estimates to analyze and correct variances?

119. Are the proposed Red Hat OpenShift project purposes different than the previously authorized Red Hat OpenShift project?

120. What does the critical path really mean?

121. Has the budget been baselined?

122. Are the quality tools and methods identified in the Quality Plan appropriate to the Red Hat OpenShift project?

123. Is the assigned Red Hat OpenShift project manager a PMP (Certified Red Hat OpenShift project manager) and experienced?

124. Have the procedures for identifying budget variances been followed?

125. What are the risks that could significantly affect procuring consultant staff for the Red Hat OpenShift project?

126. Are the people assigned to the Red Hat OpenShift project sufficiently qualified?

127. Are written status reports provided on a designated frequent basis?

128. Are the results of quality assurance reviews provided to affected groups & individuals?

129. Pop quiz – which are the same inputs as in scope planning?

2.3 Requirements Management Plan: Red Hat OpenShift

130. Why manage requirements?

131. Did you get proper approvals?

132. Are actual resource expenditures versus planned still acceptable?

133. Who will do the reporting and to whom will reports be delivered?

134. Did you avoid subjective, flowery or non-specific statements?

135. Is the change control process documented?

136. Does the Red Hat OpenShift project have a Change Control process?

137. Should you include sub-activities?

138. What is the earliest finish date for this Red Hat OpenShift project if it is scheduled to start on ...?

139. Who will approve the requirements (and if multiple approvers, in what order)?

140. After the requirements are gathered and set forth on the requirements register, theyre little more than a laundry list of items. Some may be duplicates, some might conflict with others and some will be too

broad or too vague to understand. Describe how the requirements will be analyzed. Who will perform the analysis?

141. Is any organizational data being used or stored?

142. How will unresolved questions be handled once approval has been obtained?

143. The wbs is developed as part of a joint planning session. and how do you know that youhave done this right?

144. If it exists, where is it housed?

145. Subject to change control?

146. What went right?

147. Will you perform a Requirements Risk assessment and develop a plan to deal with risks?

148. Is there formal agreement on who has authority to approve a change in requirements?

149. Is it new or replacing an existing business system or process?

2.4 Requirements Documentation: Red Hat OpenShift

150. Validity. does the system provide the functions which best support the customers needs?

151. Who is interacting with the system?

152. What are the attributes of a customer?

153. Are there any requirements conflicts?

154. How much does requirements engineering cost?

155. What is a show stopper in the requirements?

156. Are there legal issues?

157. Verifiability. can the requirements be checked?

158. Is the origin of the requirement clearly stated?

159. What images does it conjure?

160. Have the benefits identified with the system being identified clearly?

161. What kind of entity is a problem ?

162. What is the risk associated with the technology?

163. Is your business case still valid?

164. Completeness. are all functions required by the customer included?

165. What is your Elevator Speech?

166. Where do you define what is a customer, what are the attributes of customer?

167. How much testing do you need to do to prove that your system is safe?

168. Basic work/business process; high-level, what is being touched?

169. Is the requirement realistically testable?

2.5 Requirements Traceability Matrix: Red Hat OpenShift

170. What are the chronologies, contingencies, consequences, criteria?

171. Is there a requirements traceability process in place?

172. What is the WBS?

173. How do you manage scope?

174. Why use a WBS?

175. How will it affect the stakeholders personally in career?

176. Do you have a clear understanding of all subcontracts in place?

177. How small is small enough?

178. Describe the process for approving requirements so they can be added to the traceability matrix and Red Hat OpenShift project work can be performed. Will the Red Hat OpenShift project requirements become approved in writing?

179. What percentage of Red Hat OpenShift projects are producing traceability matrices between requirements and other work products?

180. Why do you manage scope?

181. Will you use a Requirements Traceability Matrix?

2.6 Project Scope Statement: Red Hat OpenShift

182. Change management vs. change leadership - what is the difference?

183. Are there adequate Red Hat OpenShift project control systems?

184. If there are vendors, have they signed off on the Red Hat OpenShift project Plan?

185. How often will scope changes be reviewed?

186. Who will you recommend approve the change, and when do you recommend the change reviews occur?

187. Are there specific processes you will use to evaluate and approve/reject changes?

188. Has everyone approved the Red Hat OpenShift projects scope statement?

189. Will all Red Hat OpenShift project issues be unconditionally tracked through the issue resolution process?

190. What are the possible consequences should a risk come to occur?

191. Will the Red Hat OpenShift project risks be managed according to the Red Hat OpenShift projects

risk management process?

192. Have you been able to easily identify success criteria and create objective measurements for each of the Red Hat OpenShift project scopes goal statements?

193. Is there a baseline plan against which to measure progress?

194. Has the Red Hat OpenShift project scope statement been reviewed as part of the baseline process?

195. Are the input requirements from the team members clearly documented and communicated?

196. Will there be a Change Control Process in place?

197. Write a brief purpose statement for this Red Hat OpenShift project. Include a business justification statement. What is the product of this Red Hat OpenShift project?

198. Is the plan for Red Hat OpenShift project resources adequate?

199. Are the meetings set up to have assigned note takers that will add action/issues to the issue list?

200. Why do you need to manage scope?

201. What actions will be taken to mitigate the risk?

2.7 Assumption and Constraint Log: Red Hat OpenShift

202. Security analysis has access to information that is sanitized?

203. What strengths do you have?

204. Is the current scope of the Red Hat OpenShift project substantially different than that originally defined in the approved Red Hat OpenShift project plan?

205. Are funding and staffing resource estimates sufficiently detailed and documented for use in planning and tracking the Red Hat OpenShift project?

206. Do the requirements meet the standards of correctness, completeness, consistency, accuracy, and readability?

207. Is there documentation of system capability requirements, data requirements, environment requirements, security requirements, and computer and hardware requirements?

208. Is the definition of the Red Hat OpenShift project scope clear; what needs to be accomplished?

209. Are there procedures in place to effectively manage interdependencies with other Red Hat OpenShift projects / systems?

210. Are there ways to reduce the time it takes to get something approved?

211. Was the document/deliverable developed per the appropriate or required standards (for example, Institute of Electrical and Electronics Engineers standards)?

212. What would you gain if you spent time working to improve this process?

213. Is the steering committee active in Red Hat OpenShift project oversight?

214. Are there unnecessary steps that are creating bottlenecks and/or causing people to wait?

215. Is the amount of effort justified by the anticipated value of forming a new process?

216. Does the system design reflect the requirements?

217. Were the system requirements formally reviewed prior to initiating the design phase?

218. Model-building: what data-analytic strategies are useful when building proportional-hazards models?

219. What is positive about the current process?

220. What does an audit system look like?

221. Are requirements management tracking tools and procedures in place?

2.8 Work Breakdown Structure: Red Hat OpenShift

222. How many levels?

223. When does it have to be done?

224. What has to be done?

225. What is the probability that the Red Hat OpenShift project duration will exceed xx weeks?

226. Is the work breakdown structure (wbs) defined and is the scope of the Red Hat OpenShift project clear with assigned deliverable owners?

227. When do you stop?

228. Do you need another level?

229. Where does it take place?

230. Why is it useful?

231. Can you make it?

232. How much detail?

233. How far down?

234. Who has to do it?

235. When would you develop a Work Breakdown

Structure?

236. How big is a work-package?

237. Why would you develop a Work Breakdown Structure?

238. Is it a change in scope?

2.9 WBS Dictionary: Red Hat OpenShift

239. Are data elements summarized through the functional organizational structure for progressively higher levels of management?

240. Are the wbs and organizational levels for application of the Red Hat OpenShift projected overhead costs identified?

241. Are data being used by managers in an effective manner to ascertain Red Hat OpenShift project or functional status, to identify reasons or significant variance, and to initiate appropriate corrective action?

242. Are overhead cost budgets established for each organization which has authority to incur overhead costs?

243. Does the scheduling system provide for the identification of work progress against technical and other milestones, and also provide for forecasts of completion dates of scheduled work?

244. Performance to date and material commitment?

245. Do work packages consist of discrete tasks which are adequately described?

246. Are current work performance indicators and goals relatable to original goals as modified by contractual changes, replanning, and reprogramming

actions?

247. Are work packages reasonably short in time duration or do they have adequate objective indicators/milestones to minimize subjectivity of the in process work evaluation?

248. Identify potential or actual overruns and underruns?

249. Are significant decision points, constraints, and interfaces identified as key milestones?

250. Identify and isolate causes of favorable and unfavorable cost and schedule variances?

251. Does the contractors system provide unit costs, equivalent unit or lot costs in terms of labor, material, other direct, and indirect costs?

252. Are estimates of costs at completion generated in a rational, consistent manner?

253. Are internal budgets for authorized, and not priced changes based on the contractors resource plan for accomplishing the work?

254. What is wrong with this Red Hat OpenShift project?

255. Does the contractors system provide for the determination of cost variances attributable to the excess usage of material?

256. Are the procedures for identifying indirect costs to incurring organizations, indirect cost pools, and

allocating the costs from the pools to the contracts formally documented?

2.10 Schedule Management Plan: Red Hat OpenShift

257. Does the Red Hat OpenShift project have a Statement of Work?

258. Are milestone deliverables effectively tracked and compared to Red Hat OpenShift project plan?

259. Has process improvement efforts been completed before requirements efforts begin?

260. Have activity relationships and interdependencies within tasks been adequately identified?

261. Are changes in scope (deliverable commitments) agreed to by all affected groups & individuals?

262. Has the business need been clearly defined?

263. Is there an issues management plan in place?

264. Is it standard practice to formally commit stakeholders to the Red Hat OpenShift project via agreements?

265. Have reserves been created to address risks?

266. Does the resource management plan include a personnel development plan?

267. Does the Red Hat OpenShift project have quality

set of schedule BOEs?

268. Is the steering committee active in Red Hat OpenShift project oversight?

269. Cost / benefit analysis?

270. Are internal Red Hat OpenShift project status meetings held at reasonable intervals?

271. Does the time Red Hat OpenShift projection include an amount for contingencies (time reserves)?

272. Have all unresolved risks been documented?

2.11 Activity List: Red Hat OpenShift

273. What is the probability the Red Hat OpenShift project can be completed in xx weeks?

274. What are the critical bottleneck activities?

275. For other activities, how much delay can be tolerated?

276. Can you determine the activity that must finish, before this activity can start?

277. What will be performed?

278. What is the total time required to complete the Red Hat OpenShift project if no delays occur?

279. Where will it be performed?

280. What are you counting on?

281. Are the required resources available or need to be acquired?

282. What went well?

283. How difficult will it be to do specific activities on this Red Hat OpenShift project?

284. What is the LF and LS for each activity?

285. How detailed should a Red Hat OpenShift project get?

286. Is infrastructure setup part of your Red Hat OpenShift project?

287. In what sequence?

288. Is there anything planned that does not need to be here?

289. Who will perform the work?

2.12 Activity Attributes: Red Hat OpenShift

290. Would you consider either of corresponding activities an outlier?

291. How else could the items be grouped?

292. Are the required resources available?

293. Have constraints been applied to the start and finish milestones for the phases?

294. Which method produces the more accurate cost assignment?

295. Has management defined a definite timeframe for the turnaround or Red Hat OpenShift project window?

296. Can more resources be added?

297. Activity: what is Missing?

298. How difficult will it be to complete specific activities on this Red Hat OpenShift project?

299. What is missing?

300. Do you feel very comfortable with your prediction?

301. Activity: fair or not fair?

302. What activity do you think you should spend the most time on?

303. Does your organization of the data change its meaning?

304. Can you re-assign any activities to another resource to resolve an over-allocation?

305. How much activity detail is required?

2.13 Milestone List: Red Hat OpenShift

306. Sustainable financial backing?

307. Loss of key staff?

308. How will you get the word out to customers?

309. Describe your organizations strengths and core competencies. What factors will make your organization succeed?

310. Calculate how long can activity be delayed?

311. Do you foresee any technical risks or developmental challenges?

312. Describe the concept of the technology, product or service that will be or has been developed. How will it be used?

313. Which path is the critical path?

314. Global influences?

315. Effects on core activities, distraction?

316. How difficult will it be to do specific activities on this Red Hat OpenShift project?

317. Milestone pages should display the UserID of the person who added the milestone. Does a report or

query exist that provides this audit information?

318. Political effects?

319. Vital contracts and partners?

320. Environmental effects?

321. Insurmountable weaknesses?

322. Continuity, supply chain robustness?

323. How soon can the activity start?

324. Who will manage the Red Hat OpenShift project on a day-to-day basis?

2.14 Network Diagram: Red Hat OpenShift

325. Are you on time?

326. What can be done concurrently?

327. How confident can you be in your milestone dates and the delivery date?

328. What activity must be completed immediately before this activity can start?

329. Why must you schedule milestones, such as reviews, throughout the Red Hat OpenShift project?

330. What must be completed before an activity can be started?

331. Planning: who, how long, what to do?

332. What job or jobs follow it?

333. Where do you schedule uncertainty time?

334. What to do and When?

335. Are the gantt chart and/or network diagram updated periodically and used to assess the overall Red Hat OpenShift project timetable?

336. What are the tools?

337. Exercise: what is the probability that the Red Hat OpenShift project duration will exceed xx weeks?

338. How difficult will it be to do specific activities on this Red Hat OpenShift project?

339. If the Red Hat OpenShift project network diagram cannot change and you have extra personnel resources, what is the BEST thing to do?

340. What is the lowest cost to complete this Red Hat OpenShift project in xx weeks?

341. What are the Key Success Factors?

342. What controls the start and finish of a job?

2.15 Activity Resource Requirements: Red Hat OpenShift

343. Other support in specific areas?

344. How many signatures do you require on a check and does this match what is in your policy and procedures?

345. Time for overtime?

346. How do you handle petty cash?

347. Are there unresolved issues that need to be addressed?

348. Anything else?

349. Why do you do that?

350. What is the Work Plan Standard?

351. Which logical relationship does the PDM use most often?

352. Do you use tools like decomposition and rolling-wave planning to produce the activity list and other outputs?

353. What are constraints that you might find during the Human Resource Planning process?

354. When does monitoring begin?

355. Organizational Applicability?

2.16 Resource Breakdown Structure: Red Hat OpenShift

356. When do they need the information?

357. Is predictive resource analysis being done?

358. What defines a successful Red Hat OpenShift project?

359. Who is allowed to perform which functions?

360. What is the purpose of assigning and documenting responsibility?

361. Who will be used as a Red Hat OpenShift project team member?

362. Who is allowed to see what data about which resources?

363. How should the information be delivered?

364. What can you do to improve productivity?

365. Who will use the system?

366. Who needs what information?

367. Who delivers the information?

368. Why do you do it?

369. What is the number one predictor of a groups productivity?

370. Which resources should be in the resource pool?

371. Changes based on input from stakeholders?

372. What is Red Hat OpenShift project communication management?

2.17 Activity Duration Estimates: Red Hat OpenShift

373. Calculate the expected duration for an activity that has a most likely time of 3, a pessimistic time of 10, and a optimiztic time of 2?

374. Do you think Red Hat OpenShift project managers of large information technology Red Hat OpenShift projects need strong technical skills?

375. What Red Hat OpenShift project was the first to use modern Red Hat OpenShift project management?

376. Why is it difficult to use Red Hat OpenShift project management software well?

377. How can software assist in Red Hat OpenShift project communications?

378. What are the advantages and disadvantages of PERT?

379. Are Red Hat OpenShift project results verified and Red Hat OpenShift project documents archived?

380. Who will promote it?

381. What is the duration of the critical path for this Red Hat OpenShift project?

382. Are changes to the scope managed according to defined procedures?

383. Do procedures exist that identify when and how human resources are introduced and removed from the Red Hat OpenShift project?

384. What are some crucial elements of a good Red Hat OpenShift project plan?

385. What are the main processes included in Red Hat OpenShift project quality management?

386. How does a Red Hat OpenShift project life cycle differ from a product life cycle?

387. Are activity dependencies documented?

388. Does a process exist to determine which risk events to accept and which events to disregard?

389. What is done after activity duration estimation?

390. Are procedures followed to ensure information is available to stakeholders in a timely manner?

391. What are two suggestions for ensuring adequate change control on Red Hat OpenShift projects that involve outside contracts?

392. Do scope statements include the Red Hat OpenShift project objectives and expected deliverables?

2.18 Duration Estimating Worksheet: Red Hat OpenShift

393. When do the individual activities need to start and finish?

394. Why estimate costs?

395. Will the Red Hat OpenShift project collaborate with the local community and leverage resources?

396. Done before proceeding with this activity or what can be done concurrently?

397. What work will be included in the Red Hat OpenShift project?

398. When does your organization expect to be able to complete it?

399. How should ongoing costs be monitored to try to keep the Red Hat OpenShift project within budget?

400. Define the work as completely as possible. What work will be included in the Red Hat OpenShift project?

401. What is next?

402. When, then?

403. Why estimate time and cost?

404. How can the Red Hat OpenShift project be displayed graphically to better visualize the activities?

405. Is a construction detail attached (to aid in explanation)?

406. Value pocket identification & quantification what are value pockets?

407. What is an Average Red Hat OpenShift project?

408. What questions do you have?

409. What utility impacts are there?

410. Can the Red Hat OpenShift project be constructed as planned?

411. What info is needed?

412. Science = process: remember the scientific method?

2.19 Project Schedule: Red Hat OpenShift

413. How much slack is available in the Red Hat OpenShift project?

414. Are quality inspections and review activities listed in the Red Hat OpenShift project schedule(s)?

415. What is the difference?

416. What documents, if any, will the subcontractor provide (eg Red Hat OpenShift project schedule, quality plan etc)?

417. How can you shorten the schedule?

418. Is Red Hat OpenShift project work proceeding in accordance with the original Red Hat OpenShift project schedule?

419. Why do you need to manage Red Hat OpenShift project Risk?

420. Is there a Schedule Management Plan that establishes the criteria and activities for developing, monitoring and controlling the Red Hat OpenShift project schedule?

421. Schedule/cost recovery?

422. Why do you need schedules?

423. What is Red Hat OpenShift project management?

424. Your Red Hat OpenShift project management plan results in a Red Hat OpenShift project schedule that is too long. If the Red Hat OpenShift project network diagram cannot change and you have extra personnel resources, what is the BEST thing to do?

425. Did the Red Hat OpenShift project come in under budget?

426. Are activities connected because logic dictates the order in which others occur?

427. Is the structure for tracking the Red Hat OpenShift project schedule well defined and assigned to a specific individual?

428. Activity charts and bar charts are graphical representations of a Red Hat OpenShift project schedule ...how do they differ?

429. How do you know that youhave done this right?

430. Verify that the update is accurate. Are all remaining durations correct?

2.20 Cost Management Plan: Red Hat OpenShift

431. Are cause and effect determined for risks when others occur?

432. Resources – how will human resources be scheduled during each phase of the Red Hat OpenShift project?

433. Is there a set of procedures defining the scope, procedures, and deliverables defining quality control?

434. Are all vendor contracts closed out?

435. Are action items captured and managed?

436. Is there general agreement & acceptance of the current status and progress of the Red Hat OpenShift project?

437. Have Red Hat OpenShift project team accountabilities & responsibilities been clearly defined?

438. Responsibilities – what is the split of responsibilities between the owner and contractors?

439. Pareto diagrams, statistical sampling, flow charting or trend analysis used quality monitoring?

440. Are all resource assumptions documented?

441. Was your organizations estimating methodology being used and followed?

442. Are estimating assumptions and constraints captured?

443. Is current scope of the Red Hat OpenShift project substantially different than that originally defined?

444. Is a pmo (Red Hat OpenShift project management office) in place and provide oversight to the Red Hat OpenShift project?

445. Schedule preparation – how will the schedules be prepared during each phase of the Red Hat OpenShift project?

2.21 Activity Cost Estimates: Red Hat OpenShift

446. Would you hire them again?

447. What is the activity recast of the budget?

448. How difficult will it be to do specific tasks on the Red Hat OpenShift project?

449. Did the Red Hat OpenShift project team have the right skills?

450. What makes a good expected result statement?

451. What procedures are put in place regarding bidding and cost comparisons, if any?

452. What areas were overlooked on this Red Hat OpenShift project?

453. Performance bond should always provide what part of the contract value?

454. What do you want to know about the stay to know if costs were inappropriately high or low?

455. Scope statement only direct or indirect costs as well?

456. Certification of actual expenditures?

457. How do you treat administrative costs in the

activity inventory?

458. Padding is bad and contingencies are good. what is the difference?

459. Estimated cost?

460. When do you enter into PPM?

461. Did the consultant work with local staff to develop local capacity?

462. Were the tasks or work products prepared by the consultant useful?

463. How do you fund change orders?

464. Can you delete activities or make them inactive?

2.22 Cost Estimating Worksheet: Red Hat OpenShift

465. What costs are to be estimated?

466. What is the estimated labor cost today based upon this information?

467. What is the purpose of estimating?

468. What happens to any remaining funds not used?

469. Ask: are others positioned to know, are others credible, and will others cooperate?

470. Will the Red Hat OpenShift project collaborate with the local community and leverage resources?

471. Who is best positioned to know and assist in identifying corresponding factors?

472. Identify the timeframe necessary to monitor progress and collect data to determine how the selected measure has changed?

473. Is the Red Hat OpenShift project responsive to community need?

474. Is it feasible to establish a control group arrangement?

475. Does the Red Hat OpenShift project provide innovative ways for stakeholders to overcome

obstacles or deliver better outcomes?

476. How will the results be shared and to whom?

477. What will others want?

478. What additional Red Hat OpenShift project(s) could be initiated as a result of this Red Hat OpenShift project?

479. What can be included?

480. Can a trend be established from historical performance data on the selected measure and are the criteria for using trend analysis or forecasting methods met?

2.23 Cost Baseline: Red Hat OpenShift

481. Is request in line with priorities?

482. What threats might prevent you from getting there?

483. Pcs for your new business. what would the life cycle costs be?

484. How long are you willing to wait before you find out were late?

485. What do you want to measure ?

486. Does the suggested change request seem to represent a necessary enhancement to the product?

487. Have you identified skills that are missing from your team?

488. Should a more thorough impact analysis be conducted?

489. What would the life cycle costs be?

490. Is there anything you need from upper management in order to be successful?

491. Has the Red Hat OpenShift project documentation been archived or otherwise disposed as described in the Red Hat OpenShift project communication plan?

492. What is the consequence?

493. Has operations management formally accepted responsibility for operating and maintaining the product(s) or service(s) delivered by the Red Hat OpenShift project?

494. Does it impact schedule, cost, quality?

495. Is the cr within Red Hat OpenShift project scope?

496. What weaknesses do you have?

497. What deliverables come first?

498. Have the actual milestone completion dates been compared to the approved schedule?

2.24 Quality Management Plan: Red Hat OpenShift

499. Do trained quality assurance auditors conduct the audits as defined in the Quality Management Plan and scheduled by the Red Hat OpenShift project manager?

500. Who else should be involved ?

501. Have all necessary approvals been obtained?

502. What are your organizations current levels and trends for the already stated measures related to employee wellbeing, satisfaction, and development?

503. Show/provide copy of procedures for taking field notes?

504. Is there a Quality Management Plan?

505. What procedures are used to determine if you use, and the number of split, replicate or duplicate samples taken at a site?

506. What data do you gather/use/compile?

507. How does your organization make it easy for customers to seek assistance or complain?

508. Are decisions/actions based on data collected?

509. Sampling part of task?

510. How do you decide what information needs to be recorded?

511. How do you ensure that your sampling methods and procedures meet your data needs?

512. How are people conducting sampling trained?

513. Who needs a qmp?

514. How is staff trained?

515. Have adequate resources been provided by management to ensure Red Hat OpenShift project success?

516. What field records are generated?

517. Does a documented Red Hat OpenShift project organizational policy & plan (i.e. governance model) exist?

2.25 Quality Metrics: Red Hat OpenShift

518. Is a risk containment plan in place?

519. How exactly do you define when differences exist?

520. Do you know how much profit a 10% decrease in waste would generate?

521. Who notifies stakeholders of normal and abnormal results?

522. What are your organizations expectations for its quality Red Hat OpenShift project?

523. The metrics–what is being considered?

524. What group is empowered to define quality requirements?

525. Is there alignment within your organization on definitions?

526. Did the team meet the Red Hat OpenShift project success criteria documented in the Quality Metrics Matrix?

527. What percentage are outcome-based?

528. If the defect rate during testing is substantially higher than that of the previous release (or a similar

product), then ask: Did you plan for and actually improve testing effectiveness?

529. Where is quality now?

530. How effective are your security tests?

531. What is the timeline to meet your goal?

532. How do you communicate results and findings to upper management?

533. What happens if you get an abnormal result?

534. Subjective quality component: customer satisfaction, how do you measure it?

535. Are applicable standards referenced and available?

536. Which report did you use to create the data you are submitting?

2.26 Process Improvement Plan: Red Hat OpenShift

537. Modeling current processes is great, and will you ever see a return on that investment?

538. The motive is determined by asking, Why do you want to achieve this goal?

539. What lessons have you learned so far?

540. How do you measure?

541. What is quality and how will you ensure it?

542. What makes people good SPI coaches?

543. Are you making progress on your improvement plan?

544. Are you making progress on the improvement framework?

545. Who should prepare the process improvement action plan?

546. Have storage and access mechanisms and procedures been determined?

547. Has the time line required to move measurement results from the points of collection to databases or users been established?

548. Does your process ensure quality?

549. Where do you focus?

550. Purpose of goal: the motive is determined by asking, why do you want to achieve this goal?

551. What personnel are the coaches for your initiative?

552. What personnel are the change agents for your initiative?

553. What personnel are the champions for the initiative?

554. What is the test-cycle concept?

555. Why quality management?

2.27 Responsibility Assignment Matrix: Red Hat OpenShift

556. Do you need to convince people that its well worth the time and effort?

557. Is the anticipated (firm and potential) business base Red Hat OpenShift projected in a rational, consistent manner?

558. Time-phased control account budgets?

559. Actual cost of work performed?

560. Does each role with Accountable responsibility have the authority within your organization to make the required decisions?

561. Are work packages assigned to performing organizations?

562. Are control accounts opened and closed based on the start and completion of work contained therein?

563. What are some important Red Hat OpenShift project communications management tools?

564. What tool can show you individual and group allocations?

565. Evaluate the impact of schedule changes, work around, etc?

566. Are too many reports done in writing instead of verbally?

567. Will too many Communicating responsibilities tangle the Red Hat OpenShift project in unnecessary communications?

568. Are indirect costs accumulated for comparison with the corresponding budgets?

569. Cwbs elements to be subcontracted, with identification of subcontractors?

570. Is budgeted cost for work performed calculated in a manner consistent with the way work is planned?

571. Is work progressively subdivided into detailed work packages as requirements are defined?

572. Do others have the time to dedicate to your Red Hat OpenShift project?

573. Does the contractors system identify work accomplishment against the schedule plan?

2.28 Roles and Responsibilities: Red Hat OpenShift

574. To decide whether to use a quality measurement, ask how will you know when it is achieved?

575. Who is involved?

576. How well did the Red Hat OpenShift project Team understand the expectations of specific roles and responsibilities?

577. Was the expectation clearly communicated?

578. What is working well?

579. Are governance roles and responsibilities documented?

580. Are Red Hat OpenShift project team roles and responsibilities identified and documented?

581. Implementation of actions: Who are the responsible units?

582. What areas would you highlight for changes or improvements?

583. Key conclusions and recommendations: Are conclusions and recommendations relevant and acceptable?

584. Influence: what areas of organizational decision

making are you able to influence when you do not have authority to make the final decision?

585. Are Red Hat OpenShift project team roles and responsibilities identified and documented?

586. Does the team have access to and ability to use data analysis tools?

587. What expectations were met?

588. Is feedback clearly communicated and non-judgmental?

589. Once the responsibilities are defined for the Red Hat OpenShift project, have the deliverables, roles and responsibilities been clearly communicated to every participant?

590. How is your work-life balance?

591. Are the quality assurance functions and related roles and responsibilities clearly defined?

592. Is the data complete?

2.29 Human Resource Management Plan: Red Hat OpenShift

593. Have all documents been archived in a Red Hat OpenShift project repository for each release?

594. How are superior performers differentiated from average performers?

595. Is stakeholder involvement adequate?

596. Are milestone deliverables effectively tracked and compared to Red Hat OpenShift project plan?

597. Is documentation created for communication with the suppliers and Vendors?

598. Did the Red Hat OpenShift project team have the right skills?

599. Is quality monitored from the perspective of the customers needs and expectations?

600. Is your organization human?

601. Has a Red Hat OpenShift project Communications Plan been developed?

602. Are vendor invoices audited for accuracy before payment?

603. How well does your organization communicate?

604. Was the scope definition used in task sequencing?

605. Have key stakeholders been identified?

606. How are you going to ensure that you have a well motivated workforce?

607. Is there general agreement & acceptance of the current status and progress of the Red Hat OpenShift project?

608. Does all Red Hat OpenShift project documentation reside in a common repository for easy access?

609. Are post milestone Red Hat OpenShift project reviews (PMPR) conducted with your organization at least once a year?

610. Is current scope of the Red Hat OpenShift project substantially different than that originally defined?

611. Are metrics used to evaluate and manage Vendors?

2.30 Communications Management Plan: Red Hat OpenShift

612. Who are the members of the governing body?

613. Will messages be directly related to the release strategy or phases of the Red Hat OpenShift project?

614. Who were proponents/opponents?

615. Do you ask; can you recommend others for you to talk with about this initiative?

616. Do you feel a register helps?

617. Can you think of other people who might have concerns or interests?

618. Are there too many who have an interest in some aspect of your work?

619. How often do you engage with stakeholders?

620. Which team member will work with each stakeholder?

621. Are stakeholders internal or external?

622. Why is stakeholder engagement important?

623. Is the stakeholder role recognized by your organization?

624. Are there common objectives between the team and the stakeholder?

625. Who did you turn to if you had questions?

626. Are others part of the communications management plan?

627. Which stakeholders can influence others?

628. Do you prepare stakeholder engagement plans?

629. Are you constantly rushing from meeting to meeting?

630. How will the person responsible for executing the communication item be notified?

631. How much time does it take to do it?

2.31 Risk Management Plan: Red Hat OpenShift

632. Are the reports useful and easy to read?

633. How quickly does each item need to be resolved?

634. What other risks are created by choosing an avoidance strategy?

635. Are enough people available?

636. How well were you able to manage your risk before?

637. Which risks should get the attention?

638. Is Red Hat OpenShift project scope stable?

639. Which is an input to the risk management process?

640. Financial risk -can your organization afford to undertake the Red Hat OpenShift project?

641. Maximize short-term return on investment?

642. How much risk can you tolerate?

643. Are status updates being made on schedule and are the updates clearly described?

644. Do requirements put excessive performance

constraints on the product?

645. What are some questions that should be addressed in a risk management plan?

646. Prioritized components/features?

647. How is the audit profession changing?

648. What is the likelihood?

649. Are testing tools available and suitable?

650. Are there new risks that mitigation strategies might introduce?

2.32 Risk Register: Red Hat OpenShift

651. Are there any knock-on effects/impact on any of the other areas?

652. Are there other alternative controls that could be implemented?

653. Assume the risk event or situation happens, what would the impact be?

654. How often will the Risk Management Plan and Risk Register be formally reviewed, and by whom?

655. What would the impact to the Red Hat OpenShift project objectives be should the risk arise?

656. Severity Prediction?

657. Are corrective measures implemented as planned?

658. Is further information required before making a decision?

659. What is the reason for current performance gaps and do the risks and opportunities identified previously account for this?

660. When will it happen?

661. Who needs to know about this?

662. What are you going to do to limit the Red Hat

OpenShift projects risk exposure due to the identified risks?

663. People risk -are people with appropriate skills available to help complete the Red Hat OpenShift project?

664. What may happen or not go according to plan?

665. Risk probability and impact: how will the probabilities and impacts of risk items be assessed?

666. What action, if any, has been taken to respond to the risk?

667. What are the major risks facing the Red Hat OpenShift project?

668. What are your key risks/show istoppers and what is being done to manage them?

669. What is a Risk?

670. How are risks graded?

2.33 Probability and Impact Assessment: Red Hat OpenShift

671. Risk data quality assessment - what is the quality of the data used to determine or assess the risk?

672. Is the process supported by tools?

673. What new technologies are being explored in the same area?

674. Is it necessary to deeply assess all Red Hat OpenShift project risks?

675. What are the preparations required for facing difficulties?

676. What are the tools and techniques used in managing the challenges faced?

677. How much is the probability of a risk occurring?

678. Supply/demand Red Hat OpenShift projections and trends; what are the levels of accuracy?

679. What are the current or emerging trends of culture?

680. What are the channels available for distribution to the customer?

681. What action do you usually take against risks?

682. What are its business ethics?

683. Assumptions analysis -what assumptions have you made or been given about your Red Hat OpenShift project?

684. How would you suggest monitoring for risk transition indicators?

685. Are the risk data complete?

686. Do you have a consistent repeatable process that is actually used?

687. Who are the international/overseas Red Hat OpenShift project partners (equipment supplier/ supplier/consultant/contractor) for this Red Hat OpenShift project?

688. How do the products attain the specifications?

689. Are trained personnel, including supervisors and Red Hat OpenShift project managers, available to handle such a large Red Hat OpenShift project?

2.34 Probability and Impact Matrix: Red Hat OpenShift

690. Does the software engineering team have the right mix of skills?

691. How likely is the current plan to come in on schedule or on budget?

692. Which role do you have in the Red Hat OpenShift project?

693. What should be done NEXT?

694. What risks were tracked?

695. What would be the effect of slippage?

696. Do you train all developers in the process?

697. Were there any Red Hat OpenShift projects similar to this one in existence?

698. Have top software and customer managers formally committed to support the Red Hat OpenShift project?

699. Have staff received necessary training?

700. Are flexibility and reuse paramount?

701. Are tools for analysis and design available?

702. Is the customer technically sophisticated in the product area?

703. What things are likely to change?

704. Are you working on the right risks?

705. What can you use the analyzed risks for?

706. My Red Hat OpenShift project leader has suddenly left your organization, what do you do?

707. Can you stabilize dynamic risk factors?

708. Do you have specific methods that you use for each phase of the process?

2.35 Risk Data Sheet: Red Hat OpenShift

709. What will be the consequences if the risk happens?

710. Is the data sufficiently specified in terms of the type of failure being analyzed, and its frequency or probability?

711. Has the most cost-effective solution been chosen?

712. Potential for recurrence?

713. What do you know?

714. Are new hazards created?

715. What is the likelihood of it happening?

716. How reliable is the data source?

717. If it happens, what are the consequences?

718. What are you trying to achieve (Objectives)?

719. What can happen?

720. Has a sensitivity analysis been carried out?

721. What are you here for (Mission)?

722. What actions can be taken to eliminate or remove risk?

723. During work activities could hazards exist?

724. Will revised controls lead to tolerable risk levels?

725. How can hazards be reduced?

726. Do effective diagnostic tests exist?

727. What is the chance that it will happen?

2.36 Procurement Management Plan: Red Hat OpenShift

728. Are adequate resources provided for the quality assurance function?

729. Has the Red Hat OpenShift project manager been identified?

730. Are status reports received per the Red Hat OpenShift project Plan?

731. Is the steering committee active in Red Hat OpenShift project oversight?

732. Are Red Hat OpenShift project contact logs kept up to date?

733. Have the key functions and capabilities been defined and assigned to each release or iteration?

734. Are key risk mitigation strategies added to the Red Hat OpenShift project schedule?

735. Was an original risk assessment/risk management plan completed?

736. Are issues raised, assessed, actioned, and resolved in a timely and efficient manner?

737. Are trade-offs between accepting the risk and mitigating the risk identified?

738. Are milestone deliverables effectively tracked and compared to Red Hat OpenShift project plan?

739. Are the people assigned to the Red Hat OpenShift project sufficiently qualified?

740. Does a documented Red Hat OpenShift project organizational policy & plan (i.e. governance model) exist?

741. Are the Red Hat OpenShift project team members located locally to the users/stakeholders?

742. Are target dates established for each milestone deliverable?

2.37 Source Selection Criteria: Red Hat OpenShift

743. What information may not be provided?

744. Does your documentation identify why the team concurs or differs with reported performance from past performance report (CPARs, questionnaire responses, etc.)?

745. How should comments received in response to a RFP be handled?

746. How long will it take for the purchase cost to be the same as the lease cost?

747. How should oral presentations be evaluated?

748. What should be considered when developing evaluation standards?

749. Who should attend debriefings?

750. What management structure does your organization consider as optimal for performing the contract?

751. What documentation is necessary regarding electronic communications?

752. Does an evaluation need to include the identification of strengths and weaknesses?

753. When is it appropriate to conduct a preproposal conference?

754. What are the special considerations for preaward debriefings?

755. What is the basis of an estimate and what assumptions were made?

756. Do you have designated specific forms or worksheets?

757. How should the oral presentations be handled?

758. Are there any common areas of weaknesses or deficiencies in the proposals in the competitive range?

759. Are responses to considerations adequate?

760. Do proposed hours support content and schedule?

761. What can not be disclosed?

762. What procedures are followed when a contractor requires access to classified information or a significant quantity of special material/information?

2.38 Stakeholder Management Plan: Red Hat OpenShift

763. Are updated Red Hat OpenShift project time & resource estimates reasonable based on the current Red Hat OpenShift project stage?

764. Have Red Hat OpenShift project team accountabilities & responsibilities been clearly defined?

765. Are all key components of a Quality Assurance Plan present?

766. Does the Red Hat OpenShift project have a Quality Culture?

767. Why would a customer be interested in a particular product or service?

768. Are meeting minutes captured and sent out after the meeting?

769. Are corrective actions and variances reported?

770. Where does the information come from?

771. Have all stakeholders been identified?

772. What sources of information are reliable?

773. What potential impact does the stakeholder have on the Red Hat OpenShift project?

774. Does the business case include how the Red Hat OpenShift project aligns with your organizations strategic goals & objectives?

775. Have stakeholder accountabilities & responsibilities been clearly defined?

776. Is the communication plan being followed?

777. How many Red Hat OpenShift project staff does this specific process affect?

778. Have Red Hat OpenShift project success criteria been defined?

779. How are stakeholders chosen and what roles might they have on a Red Hat OpenShift project?

780. Are decisions captured in a decisions log?

2.39 Change Management Plan: Red Hat OpenShift

781. What are the major changes to processes?

782. Readiness -what is a successful end state?

783. Do the proposed users have access to the appropriate documentation?

784. Has this been negotiated with the customer and sponsor?

785. Will the culture embrace or reject this change?

786. What risks may occur upfront?

787. What is the negative impact of communicating too soon or too late?

788. Who will be the change levers?

789. What work practices will be affected?

790. What are the dependencies?

791. What provokes organizational change?

792. What is the reason for the communication?

793. Have the approved procedures and policies been published?

794. What is going to be done differently?

795. Are there any restrictions on who can receive the communications?

796. Have the systems been configured and tested?

797. Is there a support model for this application and are the details available for distribution?

798. Do there need to be new channels developed?

799. Impact of systems implementation on organization change?

3.0 Executing Process Group: Red Hat OpenShift

800. What are the main types of contracts if you do decide to outsource?

801. In what way has the program come up with innovative measures for problem-solving?

802. Are escalated issues resolved promptly?

803. Will additional funds be needed for hardware or software?

804. How will professionals learn what is expected from them what the deliverables are?

805. Could a new application negatively affect the current IT infrastructure?

806. What are the key components of the Red Hat OpenShift project communications plan?

807. Measurable - are the targets measurable?

808. How will you know you did it?

809. After how many days will the lease cost be the same as the purchase cost for the equipment?

810. What business situation is being addressed?

811. Does the Red Hat OpenShift project team have

enough people to execute the Red Hat OpenShift project plan?

812. Are decisions made in a timely manner?

813. What does it mean to take a systems view of a Red Hat OpenShift project?

814. What areas does the group agree are the biggest success on the Red Hat OpenShift project?

815. What are deliverables of your Red Hat OpenShift project?

816. Based on your Red Hat OpenShift project communication management plan, what worked well?

817. Who will provide training?

3.1 Team Member Status Report: Red Hat OpenShift

818. How can you make it practical?

819. Is there evidence that staff is taking a more professional approach toward management of your organizations Red Hat OpenShift projects?

820. Do you have an Enterprise Red Hat OpenShift project Management Office (EPMO)?

821. What is to be done?

822. How it is to be done?

823. How will resource planning be done?

824. When a teams productivity and success depend on collaboration and the efficient flow of information, what generally fails them?

825. Why is it to be done?

826. How much risk is involved?

827. The problem with Reward & Recognition Programs is that the truly deserving people all too often get left out. How can you make it practical?

828. Are the attitudes of staff regarding Red Hat OpenShift project work improving?

829. Does the product, good, or service already exist within your organization?

830. Will the staff do training or is that done by a third party?

831. Are the products of your organizations Red Hat OpenShift projects meeting customers objectives?

832. Does every department have to have a Red Hat OpenShift project Manager on staff?

833. Are your organizations Red Hat OpenShift projects more successful over time?

834. What specific interest groups do you have in place?

835. How does this product, good, or service meet the needs of the Red Hat OpenShift project and your organization as a whole?

836. Does your organization have the means (staff, money, contract, etc.) to produce or to acquire the product, good, or service?

3.2 Change Request: Red Hat OpenShift

837. What is the function of the change control committee?

838. How do you get changes (code) out in a timely manner?

839. Describe how modifications, enhancements, defects and/or deficiencies shall be notified (e.g. Problem Reports, Change Requests etc) and managed. Detail warranty and/or maintenance periods?

840. How shall the implementation of changes be recorded?

841. When do you create a change request?

842. What is the relationship between requirements attributes and attributes like complexity and size?

843. Screen shots or attachments included in a Change Request?

844. Has a formal technical review been conducted to assess technical correctness?

845. Who can suggest changes?

846. How is the change documented (format, content, storage)?

847. Can static requirements change attributes like the size of the change be used to predict reliability in execution?

848. How to get changes (code) out in a timely manner?

849. Are there requirements attributes that are strongly related to the complexity and size?

850. For which areas does this operating procedure apply?

851. What are the requirements for urgent changes?

852. How can you ensure that changes have been made properly?

853. Who needs to approve change requests?

854. Are change requests logged and managed?

3.3 Change Log: Red Hat OpenShift

855. How does this change affect the timeline of the schedule?

856. Do the described changes impact on the integrity or security of the system?

857. Is the requested change request a result of changes in other Red Hat OpenShift project(s)?

858. Is the change backward compatible without limitations?

859. Is the change request within Red Hat OpenShift project scope?

860. Who initiated the change request?

861. Is this a mandatory replacement?

862. When was the request submitted?

863. Is the change request open, closed or pending?

864. Will the Red Hat OpenShift project fail if the change request is not executed?

865. When was the request approved?

866. Where do changes come from?

867. How does this relate to the standards developed for specific business processes?

868. How does this change affect scope?

869. Does the suggested change request represent a desired enhancement to the products functionality?

870. Is the submitted change a new change or a modification of a previously approved change?

3.4 Decision Log: Red Hat OpenShift

871. Decision-making process; how will the team make decisions?

872. Is your opponent open to a non-traditional workflow, or will it likely challenge anything you do?

873. Is everything working as expected?

874. How do you know when you are achieving it?

875. How consolidated and comprehensive a story can you tell by capturing currently available incident data in a central location and through a log of key decisions during an incident?

876. How does the use a Decision Support System influence the strategies/tactics or costs?

877. It becomes critical to track and periodically revisit both operational effectiveness; Are you noticing all that you need to, and are you interpreting what you see effectively?

878. How does provision of information, both in terms of content and presentation, influence acceptance of alternative strategies?

879. Does anything need to be adjusted?

880. With whom was the decision shared or considered?

881. What are the cost implications?

882. What alternatives/risks were considered?

883. What makes you different or better than others companies selling the same thing?

884. Adversarial environment. is your opponent open to a non-traditional workflow, or will it likely challenge anything you do?

885. How does an increasing emphasis on cost containment influence the strategies and tactics used?

886. How effective is maintaining the log at facilitating organizational learning?

887. What eDiscovery problem or issue did your organization set out to fix or make better?

888. Which variables make a critical difference?

889. At what point in time does loss become unacceptable?

890. What is the average size of your matters in an applicable measurement?

3.5 Quality Audit: Red Hat OpenShift

891. Is the process of self review, learning and improvement endemic throughout your organization?

892. How does your organization know that its Mission, Vision and Values Statements are appropriate and effectively guiding your organization?

893. How does your organization know that it is appropriately effective and constructive in preparing its staff for organizational aspirations?

894. Health and safety arrangements; stress management workshops. How does your organization know that it provides a safe and healthy environment?

895. How does your organization know that its advisory services are appropriately effective and constructive?

896. What experience do staff have in the type of work that the audit entails?

897. How does your organization know that its staffing profile is optimally aligned with the capability requirements implicit (or explicit) in its Strategic Plan?

898. Is there any content that may be legally actionable?

899. How does your organization know that its management system is appropriately effective and

constructive?

900. Is there a risk that information provided by management may not always be reliable?

901. How does your organization know that the research supervision provided to its staff is appropriately effective and constructive?

902. How do staff know if they are doing a good job?

903. How well do you think your organization engages with the outside community?

904. How does your organization know that it provides a safe and healthy environment?

905. How does your organization know that its system for inducting new staff to maximize workplace contributions are appropriately effective and constructive?

906. Are the review comments incorporated?

907. What are you trying to do?

908. How does your organization know that its system for examining work done is appropriately effective and constructive?

909. How does your organization know that its system for attending to the particular needs of its international staff is appropriately effective and constructive?

910. Is refuse and garbage adequately stored and

disposed of with sufficient frequency to prevent contamination?

3.6 Team Directory: Red Hat OpenShift

911. Who will talk to the customer?

912. Decisions: what could be done better to improve the quality of the constructed product?

913. Days from the time the issue is identified?

914. How does the team resolve conflicts and ensure tasks are completed?

915. How will you accomplish and manage the objectives?

916. Who will report Red Hat OpenShift project status to all stakeholders?

917. Where will the product be used and/or delivered or built when appropriate?

918. Who will be the stakeholders on your next Red Hat OpenShift project?

919. How and in what format should information be presented?

920. Process decisions: how well was task order work performed?

921. Who are the Team Members?

922. When does information need to be distributed?

923. Who should receive information (all stakeholders)?

924. Decisions: is the most suitable form of contract being used?

925. Do purchase specifications and configurations match requirements?

926. Who are your stakeholders (customers, sponsors, end users, team members)?

927. Process decisions: which organizational elements and which individuals will be assigned management functions?

928. Process decisions: are contractors adequately prosecuting the work?

3.7 Team Operating Agreement: Red Hat OpenShift

929. How do you want to be thought of and known within your organization?

930. Do you brief absent members after they view meeting notes or listen to a recording?

931. What is the number of cases currently teamed?

932. Do team members need to frequently communicate as a full group to make timely decisions?

933. What are the current caseload numbers in the unit?

934. Do you ask participants to close laptops and place mobile devices on silent on the table while the meeting is in progress?

935. Are there the right people on your team?

936. Confidentiality: how will confidential information be handled?

937. Do you determine the meeting length and time of day?

938. Do you ensure that all participants know how to use the required technology?

939. Must your members collaborate successfully to complete Red Hat OpenShift projects?

940. Do you solicit member feedback about meetings and what would make them better?

941. Does your team need access to all documents and information at all times?

942. What is a Virtual Team?

943. Are there influences outside the team that may affect performance, and if so, have you identified and addressed them?

944. What is group supervision?

945. What types of accommodations will be formulated and put in place for sustaining the team?

946. What is the anticipated procedure (recruitment, solicitation of volunteers, or assignment) for selecting team members?

947. Are there differences in access to communication and collaboration technology based on team member location?

948. Do you use a parking lot for any items that are important and outside of the agenda?

3.8 Team Performance Assessment: Red Hat OpenShift

949. To what degree does the teams purpose constitute a broader, deeper aspiration than just accomplishing short-term goals?

950. What is method variance?

951. To what degree will team members, individually and collectively, commit time to help themselves and others learn and develop skills?

952. Can familiarity breed backup?

953. To what degree is the team cognizant of small wins to be celebrated along the way?

954. Do you give group members authority to make at least some important decisions?

955. To what degree are the teams goals and objectives clear, simple, and measurable?

956. To what degree do members articulate the goals beyond the team membership?

957. Is there a particular method of data analysis that you would recommend as a means of demonstrating that method variance is not of great concern for a given dataset?

958. To what degree are the members clear on what

they are individually responsible for and what they are jointly responsible for?

959. Effects of crew composition on crew performance: Does the whole equal the sum of its parts?

960. What are you doing specifically to develop the leaders around you?

961. To what degree will the team adopt a concrete, clearly understood, and agreed-upon approach that will result in achievement of the teams goals?

962. Where to from here?

963. To what degree are the skill areas critical to team performance present?

964. To what degree does the teams purpose contain themes that are particularly meaningful and memorable?

965. If you have received criticism from reviewers that your work suffered from method variance, what was the circumstance?

966. To what degree does the teams work approach provide opportunity for members to engage in results-based evaluation?

967. To what degree can all members engage in open and interactive considerations?

968. To what degree are the relative importance and priority of the goals clear to all team members?

3.9 Team Member Performance Assessment: Red Hat OpenShift

969. Did training work?

970. How do you create a self-sustaining capacity for a collaborative culture?

971. How should adaptive assessments be implemented?

972. How is assessment information achieved, stored?

973. What are best practices for delivering and developing training evaluations to maximize the benefits of leveraging emerging technologies?

974. What, if any, steps are available for employees who feel they have been unfairly or inaccurately rated?

975. How do you make use of research?

976. To what degree are sub-teams possible or necessary?

977. To what degree do team members feel that the purpose of the team is important, if not exciting?

978. Goals met?

979. What makes them effective?

980. Do the goals support your organizations goals?

981. How do you currently account for your results in the teams achievement?

982. What happens if a team member receives a Rating of Unsatisfactory?

983. How do you use data to inform instruction and improve staff achievement?

984. Are any validation activities performed?

985. How do you know that all team members are learning?

986. To what extent did the evaluation influence the instructional path, such as with adaptive testing?

3.10 Issue Log: Red Hat OpenShift

987. Who needs to know and how much?

988. Who do you turn to if you have questions?

989. What help do you and your team need from the stakeholders?

990. Is access to the Issue Log controlled?

991. Are the stakeholders getting the information they need, are they consulted, are concerns addressed?

992. Which stakeholders are thought leaders, influences, or early adopters?

993. What effort will a change need?

994. Is there an important stakeholder who is actively opposed and will not receive messages?

995. What approaches to you feel are the best ones to use?

996. Who is involved as you identify stakeholders?

997. How do you manage communications?

998. Is the issue log kept in a safe place?

999. Who reported the issue?

1000. What are the typical contents?

1001. How is this initiative related to other portfolios, programs, or Red Hat OpenShift projects?

4.0 Monitoring and Controlling Process Group: Red Hat OpenShift

1002. How to ensure validity, quality and consistency?

1003. Is there adequate validation on required fields?

1004. Based on your Red Hat OpenShift project communication management plan, what worked well?

1005. Are the services being delivered?

1006. How well did the chosen processes fit the needs of the Red Hat OpenShift project?

1007. Key stakeholders to work with. How many potential communications channels exist on the Red Hat OpenShift project?

1008. How are you doing?

1009. Change, where should you look for problems?

1010. Do the partners have sufficient financial capacity to keep up the benefits produced by the programme?

1011. Propriety: who needs to be involved in the evaluation to be ethical?

1012. Specific - is the objective clear in terms of what, how, when, and where the situation will be changed?

1013. Are the necessary foundations in place to ensure the sustainability of the results of the programme?

1014. What will you do to minimize the impact should a risk event occur?

1015. Is there sufficient time allotted between the general system design and the detailed system design phases?

1016. Purpose: toward what end is the evaluation being conducted?

1017. User: who wants the information and what are they interested in?

1018. How well did the team follow the chosen processes?

1019. Were escalated issues resolved promptly?

4.1 Project Performance Report: Red Hat OpenShift

1020. To what degree do team members articulate the teams work approach?

1021. What is the degree to which rules govern information exchange between groups?

1022. To what degree will each member have the opportunity to advance his or her professional skills in all three of the above categories while contributing to the accomplishment of the teams purpose and goals?

1023. To what degree is there centralized control of information sharing?

1024. What is the PRS?

1025. To what degree does the funding match the requirement?

1026. To what degree will new and supplemental skills be introduced as the need is recognized?

1027. To what degree does the formal organization make use of individual resources and meet individual needs?

1028. To what degree are fresh input and perspectives systematically caught and added (for example, through information and analysis, new members, and senior sponsors)?

1029. To what degree do team members understand one anothers roles and skills?

1030. To what degree does the teams work approach provide opportunity for members to engage in fact-based problem solving?

1031. To what degree does the informal organization make use of individual resources and meet individual needs?

1032. To what degree does the information network communicate information relevant to the task?

1033. To what degree will the team ensure that all members equitably share the work essential to the success of the team?

1034. What is in it for you?

1035. How can Red Hat OpenShift project sustainability be maintained?

4.2 Variance Analysis: Red Hat OpenShift

1036. Who are responsible for the establishment of budgets and assignment of resources for overhead performance?

1037. Does the scheduling system identify in a timely manner the status of work?

1038. How does your organization measure performance?

1039. Are the actual costs used for variance analysis reconcilable with data from the accounting system?

1040. Are there changes in the overhead pool and/or organization structures?

1041. Is the entire contract planned in time-phased control accounts to the extent practicable?

1042. How are material, labor, and overhead standards set?

1043. How have the setting and use of standards changed over time?

1044. What is exceptional?

1045. How do you manage changes in the nature of the overhead requirements?

1046. What can be the cause of an increase in costs?

1047. Why do variances exist?

1048. How does the use of a single conversion element (rather than the traditional labor and overhead elements) affect standard costing?

1049. What does an unfavorable overhead volume variance mean?

1050. Is there a logical explanation for any variance?

1051. Did an existing competitor change strategy?

4.3 Earned Value Status: Red Hat OpenShift

1052. How does this compare with other Red Hat OpenShift projects?

1053. What is the unit of forecast value?

1054. How much is it going to cost by the finish?

1055. Where are your problem areas?

1056. Are you hitting your Red Hat OpenShift projects targets?

1057. Where is evidence-based earned value in your organization reported?

1058. Verification is a process of ensuring that the developed system satisfies the stakeholders agreements and specifications; Are you building the product right? What do you verify?

1059. Earned value can be used in almost any Red Hat OpenShift project situation and in almost any Red Hat OpenShift project environment. it may be used on large Red Hat OpenShift projects, medium sized Red Hat OpenShift projects, tiny Red Hat OpenShift projects (in cut-down form), complex and simple Red Hat OpenShift projects and in any market sector. some people, of course, know all about earned value, they have used it for years - but perhaps not as effectively as they could have?

1060. When is it going to finish?

1061. Validation is a process of ensuring that the developed system will actually achieve the stakeholders desired outcomes; Are you building the right product? What do you validate?

1062. If earned value management (EVM) is so good in determining the true status of a Red Hat OpenShift project and Red Hat OpenShift project its completion, why is it that hardly any one uses it in information systems related Red Hat OpenShift projects?

4.4 Risk Audit: Red Hat OpenShift

1063. How will you maximise opportunities?

1064. Is safety information provided to all involved?

1065. What effect would a better risk management program have had?

1066. Does your auditor understand your business?

1067. Estimated size of product in number of programs, files, transactions?

1068. Are duties out-of-class?

1069. Where will the next scandal or adverse media involving your organization come from?

1070. What expertise does the Board have on quality, outcomes, and errors?

1071. What are the outcomes you are looking for?

1072. Will participants be required to sign a legally counselled waiver or risk disclaimer when entering an event?

1073. To what extent should analytical procedures be utilized in the risk-assessment process?

1074. Do the people have the right combinations of skills?

1075. Risks with Red Hat OpenShift projects or new initiatives?

1076. Will safety checks of personal equipment supplied by competitors be conducted?

1077. Have customers been involved fully in the definition of requirements?

1078. Are regular safety inspections made of buildings, grounds and equipment?

1079. Which assets are important?

4.5 Contractor Status Report: Red Hat OpenShift

1080. How is risk transferred?

1081. Are there contractual transfer concerns?

1082. How does the proposed individual meet each requirement?

1083. What was the actual budget or estimated cost for your organizations services?

1084. Describe how often regular updates are made to the proposed solution. Are corresponding regular updates included in the standard maintenance plan?

1085. What was the final actual cost?

1086. What are the minimum and optimal bandwidth requirements for the proposed solution?

1087. What process manages the contracts?

1088. What was the budget or estimated cost for your organizations services?

1089. What is the average response time for answering a support call?

1090. Who can list a Red Hat OpenShift project as organization experience, your organization or a previous employee of your organization?

1091. How long have you been using the services?

1092. If applicable; describe your standard schedule for new software version releases. Are new software version releases included in the standard maintenance plan?

1093. What was the overall budget or estimated cost?

4.6 Formal Acceptance: Red Hat OpenShift

1094. How well did the team follow the methodology?

1095. Do you perform formal acceptance or burn-in tests?

1096. Do you buy pre-configured systems or build your own configuration?

1097. Did the Red Hat OpenShift project manager and team act in a professional and ethical manner?

1098. What can you do better next time?

1099. What lessons were learned about your Red Hat OpenShift project management methodology?

1100. General estimate of the costs and times to complete the Red Hat OpenShift project?

1101. How does your team plan to obtain formal acceptance on your Red Hat OpenShift project?

1102. What are the requirements against which to test, Who will execute?

1103. Does it do what client said it would?

1104. Was the client satisfied with the Red Hat OpenShift project results?

1105. Was the sponsor/customer satisfied?

1106. Was the Red Hat OpenShift project goal achieved?

1107. What features, practices, and processes proved to be strengths or weaknesses?

1108. Who would use it?

1109. What is the Acceptance Management Process?

1110. Do you buy-in installation services?

1111. Who supplies data?

1112. What function(s) does it fill or meet?

1113. Have all comments been addressed?

5.0 Closing Process Group: Red Hat OpenShift

1114. What is an Encumbrance?

1115. If a risk event occurs, what will you do?

1116. How well defined and documented were the Red Hat OpenShift project management processes you chose to use?

1117. Did the Red Hat OpenShift project team have the right skills?

1118. Is this a follow-on to a previous Red Hat OpenShift project?

1119. Based on your Red Hat OpenShift project communication management plan, what worked well?

1120. What is the overall risk of the Red Hat OpenShift project to your organization?

1121. What were things that you need to improve?

1122. What were the desired outcomes?

1123. How well did the chosen processes produce the expected results?

1124. Did you do things well?

1125. How critical is the Red Hat OpenShift project success to the success of your organization?

1126. What areas were overlooked on this Red Hat OpenShift project?

1127. What is the risk of failure to your organization?

5.1 Procurement Audit: Red Hat OpenShift

1128. Is the chosen supplier part of your organizations database?

1129. Are prices always included on the purchase order?

1130. Relevance of the contract to the Internal Market?

1131. Proper and complete records of transactions and events are maintained?

1132. Has the award included no items different from the already stated contained in bid specifications?

1133. Did the conditions of contract comply with the detail provided in the procurement documents and with the outcome of the procurement procedure followed?

1134. Are advantages and disadvantages of in-house production, outsourcing and Public Private Partnerships considered?

1135. Do your organizations policies promote and/or safeguard fair competition?

1136. Are there systems for recording and monitoring in order to discover malpractice and fraud in the procurement function/unit?

1137. What are your ethical guidelines for public procurement?

1138. Are obtained prices/qualities competitive to prices/qualities obtained by other procurement functions/units, comparing obtained or improved value for money?

1139. Must the receipt of goods be approved prior to payment?

1140. Are controls proportionated to risks?

1141. Did you consider and evaluate alternatives, like bundling needs with other departments or grouping supplies in separate lots with different characteristics?

1142. Were the specifications of the contract determined free from influence of particular interests of consultants, experts or other economic operators?

1143. Are required quality and service standards set?

1144. Are open purchase orders with a fixed monetary limitation used for local purchases of small dollar value?

1145. Does the procurement function/unit understand costumer needs, supply markets and suppliers?

1146. Are there regular reviews and analysis of the performance of the procurement function/unit?

1147. Were any additional works or deliveries

admissible, without recourse to a new procurement procedure?

5.2 Contract Close-Out: Red Hat OpenShift

1148. Have all acceptance criteria been met prior to final payment to contractors?

1149. What happens to the recipient of services?

1150. How does it work?

1151. Was the contract type appropriate?

1152. Change in circumstances?

1153. Why Outsource?

1154. How/when used ?

1155. Was the contract complete without requiring numerous changes and revisions?

1156. What is capture management?

1157. Parties: who is involved?

1158. Change in knowledge?

1159. Parties: Authorized?

1160. Have all contract records been included in the Red Hat OpenShift project archives?

1161. Are the signers the authorized officials?

1162. Was the contract sufficiently clear so as not to result in numerous disputes and misunderstandings?

1163. Have all contracts been completed?

1164. Has each contract been audited to verify acceptance and delivery?

1165. Have all contracts been closed?

1166. Change in attitude or behavior?

1167. How is the contracting office notified of the automatic contract close-out?

5.3 Project or Phase Close-Out: Red Hat OpenShift

1168. What are the mandatory communication needs for each stakeholder?

1169. Who are the Red Hat OpenShift project stakeholders and what are roles and involvement?

1170. In addition to assessing whether the Red Hat OpenShift project was successful, it is equally critical to analyze why it was or was not fully successful. Are you including this?

1171. What information is each stakeholder group interested in?

1172. When and how were information needs best met?

1173. What information did each stakeholder need to contribute to the Red Hat OpenShift projects success?

1174. Which changes might a stakeholder be required to make as a result of the Red Hat OpenShift project?

1175. Is there a clear cause and effect between the activity and the lesson learned?

1176. If you were the Red Hat OpenShift project sponsor, how would you determine which Red Hat OpenShift project team(s) and/or individuals deserve recognition?

1177. Does the lesson educate others to improve performance?

1178. Complete yes or no?

1179. What could have been improved?

1180. What advantages do the an individual interview have over a group meeting, and vice-versa?

1181. What are the marketing communication needs for each stakeholder?

1182. What can you do better next time, and what specific actions can you take to improve?

1183. Does the lesson describe a function that would be done differently the next time?

1184. What process was planned for managing issues/risks?

1185. Were the outcomes different from the already stated planned?

5.4 Lessons Learned: Red Hat OpenShift

1186. What Red Hat OpenShift project circumstances were not anticipated?

1187. What were the challenges and pitfalls?

1188. What policy constraints are relevant?

1189. Overall, how effective was the performance of the Red Hat OpenShift project Manager?

1190. Who needs to learn lessons?

1191. Is the lesson based on actual Red Hat OpenShift project experience rather than on independent research?

1192. How efficient and effective were Red Hat OpenShift project team meetings?

1193. What is the expected lifespan of the deliverable?

1194. What could be done to improve the process?

1195. What data are likely to be missing?

1196. How objective was the collection of data?

1197. To what extent was the evolution of risks communicated?

1198. How effective were Best Practices & Lessons Learned from prior Red Hat OpenShift projects utilized in this Red Hat OpenShift project?

1199. What things surprised you on the Red Hat OpenShift project that were not in the plan?

1200. What other questions should you have asked?

1201. What were the main bottlenecks on the process?

1202. How useful was your testing?

1203. How well were your expectations met regarding the extent of your involvement in the Red Hat OpenShift project (effort, time commitments, etc.)?

1204. What is the impact of tax policy?

1205. What would you change?

Red Hat OpenShift and Managing Projects, Criteria for Project Managers:

1.0 Initiating Process Group: Red Hat OpenShift

1. Contingency planning. if a risk event occurs, what will you do?

2. Will the Red Hat OpenShift project meet the client requirements, and will it achieve the business success criteria that justified doing the Red Hat OpenShift project in the first place?

3. Measurable - are the targets measurable?

4. How will you know you did it?

5. Mitigate. what will you do to minimize the impact should the risk event occur?

6. What will you do?

7. What were things that you did well, and could improve, and how?

8. Establishment of pm office?

9. Who are the Red Hat OpenShift project stakeholders?

10. The Red Hat OpenShift project you are managing has nine stakeholders. How many channel of communications are there between corresponding stakeholders?

11. What is the NEXT thing to do?

12. If the risk event occurs, what will you do?

13. Are the Red Hat OpenShift project team and stakeholders meeting regularly and using a meeting agenda and taking notes to accurately document what is being covered and what happened in the weekly meetings?

14. What will you do to minimize the impact should a risk event occur?

15. Were decisions made in a timely manner?

16. Are you certain deliverables are properly completed and meet quality standards?

17. What must be done?

18. During which stage of Risk planning are risks prioritized based on probability and impact?

19. Were sponsors and decision makers available when needed outside regularly scheduled meetings?

1.1 Project Charter: Red Hat OpenShift

20. How are Red Hat OpenShift projects different from operations?

21. Are there special technology requirements?

22. Is it an improvement over existing products?

23. What is the business need?

24. What changes can you make to improve?

25. Are you building in-house ?

26. What are the constraints?

27. Who ise input and support will this Red Hat OpenShift project require?

28. What ideas do you have for initial tests of change (PDSA cycles)?

29. Name and describe the elements that deal with providing the detail?

30. What is in it for you?

31. Customer: who are you doing the Red Hat OpenShift project for?

32. How will you know that a change is an

improvement?

33. What are the assigned resources?

34. Must Have?

35. Why is a Red Hat OpenShift project Charter used?

36. Strategic fit: what is the strategic initiative identifier for this Red Hat OpenShift project?

37. Who manages integration?

38. How will you know a change is an improvement?

39. Assumptions and constraints: what assumptions were made in defining the Red Hat OpenShift project?

1.2 Stakeholder Register: Red Hat OpenShift

40. What is the power of the stakeholder?

41. What & Why?

42. How much influence do they have on the Red Hat OpenShift project?

43. Who is managing stakeholder engagement?

44. How will reports be created?

45. Who wants to talk about Security?

46. How big is the gap?

47. Is your organization ready for change?

48. Who are the stakeholders?

49. What are the major Red Hat OpenShift project milestones requiring communications or providing communications opportunities?

50. How should employers make voices heard?

51. What opportunities exist to provide communications?

1.3 Stakeholder Analysis Matrix: Red Hat OpenShift

52. How to measure the achievement of the Development Objective?

53. Who is influential in the Red Hat OpenShift project area (both thematic and geographic areas)?

54. Do recommendations include actions to address any differential distribution of impacts?

55. Disadvantages of proposition?

56. How to measure the achievement of the Outputs?

57. What is the stakeholders mandate, what is mission?

58. Resource providers; who can provide resources to ensure the implementation of the Red Hat OpenShift project?

59. Who is most dependent on the resources at stake?

60. Management cover, succession?

61. What are the mechanisms of public and social accountability, and how can they be made better?

62. Who will be affected by the Red Hat OpenShift project?

63. Will the impacts be local, national or international?

64. What is your organizations competitors doing?

65. Which resources are required?

66. Are you working on the right risks?

67. Inoculations or payment to receive them?

68. Morale, commitment, leadership?

69. Market developments?

70. What do your organizations stakeholders do better than anyone else?

71. Loss of key staff?

2.0 Planning Process Group: Red Hat OpenShift

72. Are the follow-up indicators relevant and do they meet the quality needed to measure the outputs and outcomes of the Red Hat OpenShift project?

73. To what extent and in what ways are the Red Hat OpenShift project contributing to progress towards organizational reform?

74. What should you do next?

75. Are the necessary foundations in place to ensure the sustainability of the results of the Red Hat OpenShift project?

76. Is the duration of the program sufficient to ensure a cycle that will Red Hat OpenShift project the sustainability of the interventions?

77. The Red Hat OpenShift project charter is created in which Red Hat OpenShift project management process group?

78. Professionals want to know what is expected from them; what are the deliverables?

79. If action is called for, what form should it take?

80. To what extent have public/private national resources and/or counterparts been mobilized to contribute to the programs objective and produce

results and impacts?

81. How many days can task X be late in starting without affecting the Red Hat OpenShift project completion date?

82. Are there efficient coordination mechanisms to avoid overloading the counterparts, participating stakeholders?

83. Does it make any difference if you are successful?

84. Product breakdown structure (pbs): what is the Red Hat OpenShift project result or product, and how should it look like, what are its parts?

85. You did your readings, yes?

86. How will it affect you?

87. To what extent is the program helping to influence your organizations policy framework?

88. Have more efficient (sensitive) and appropriate measures been adopted to respond to the political and socio-cultural problems identified?

89. To what extent do the intervention objectives and strategies of the Red Hat OpenShift project respond to your organizations plans?

90. To what extent have the target population and participants made the activities own, taking an active role in it?

91. In which Red Hat OpenShift project management

process group is the detailed Red Hat OpenShift
project budget created?

2.1 Project Management Plan: Red Hat OpenShift

92. Will you add a schedule and diagram?

93. Are calculations and results of analyzes essentially correct?

94. What goes into your Red Hat OpenShift project Charter?

95. What is Red Hat OpenShift project scope management?

96. Has the selected plan been formulated using cost effectiveness and incremental analysis techniques?

97. Are alternatives safe, functional, constructible, economical, reasonable and sustainable?

98. Are comparable cost estimates used for comparing, screening and selecting alternative plans, and has a reasonable cost estimate been developed for the recommended plan?

99. What would you do differently what did not work?

100. What data/reports/tools/etc. do your PMs need?

101. Where does all this information come from?

102. What happened during the process that you found interesting?

103. What went right?

104. What should you drop in order to add something new?

105. If the Red Hat OpenShift project management plan is a comprehensive document that guides you in Red Hat OpenShift project execution and control, then what should it NOT contain?

106. Does the selected plan protect privacy?

107. When is a Red Hat OpenShift project management plan created?

108. How well are you able to manage your risk?

109. Are the existing and future without-plan conditions reasonable and appropriate?

2.2 Scope Management Plan: Red Hat OpenShift

110. When is corrective or preventative action required?

111. Are staff skills known and available for each task?

112. Assess the expected stability of the scope of this Red Hat OpenShift project how likely is it to change, how frequently, and by how much?

113. Organizational policies that might affect the availability of resources?

114. Is there an on-going process in place to monitor Red Hat OpenShift project risks?

115. Is there a formal process for updating the Red Hat OpenShift project baseline?

116. What are the risks of not having good inter-organization cooperation on the Red Hat OpenShift project?

117. Did your Red Hat OpenShift project ask for this?

118. Have Red Hat OpenShift project success criteria been defined?

119. Has a sponsor been identified?

120. Are assumptions being identified, recorded,

analyzed, qualified and closed?

121. Timeline and milestones?

122. Where do scope management processes fit in?

123. Are there procedures in place to effectively manage interdependencies with other Red Hat OpenShift projects, systems, Vendors and your organizations work effort?

124. Are written status reports provided on a designated frequent basis?

125. Are cause and effect determined for risks when they occur?

126. How many changes are you making?

127. What weaknesses do you have?

128. Are corrective actions taken when actual results are substantially different from detailed Red Hat OpenShift project plan (variances)?

2.3 Requirements Management Plan: Red Hat OpenShift

129. Will the product release be stable and mature enough to be deployed in the user community?

130. Why manage requirements?

131. Did you get proper approvals?

132. Is requirements work dependent on any other specific Red Hat OpenShift project or non-Red Hat OpenShift project activities (e.g. funding, approvals, procurement)?

133. What information regarding the Red Hat OpenShift project requirements will be reported?

134. How often will the reporting occur?

135. Are actual resources expenditures versus planned expenditures acceptable?

136. Who will perform the analysis?

137. Has the requirements team been instructed in the Change Control process?

138. Do you really need to write this document at all?

139. How will the information be distributed?

140. Is the system software (non-operating system)

new to the IT Red Hat OpenShift project team?

141. Do you understand the role that each stakeholder will play in the requirements process?

142. How will you communicate scheduled tasks to other team members?

143. How do you know that you have done this right?

144. Who will do the reporting and to whom will reports be delivered?

145. Is the user satisfied?

146. Who has the authority to reject Red Hat OpenShift project requirements?

147. How will bidders price evaluations be done, by deliverables, phases, or in a big bang?

148. What cost metrics will be used?

2.4 Requirements Documentation: Red Hat OpenShift

149. What is the risk associated with cost and schedule?

150. How much testing do you need to do to prove that your system is safe?

151. Do your constraints stand?

152. If applicable; are there issues linked with the fact that this is an offshore Red Hat OpenShift project?

153. How will requirements be documented and who signs off on them?

154. Who is interacting with the system?

155. How do you get the user to tell you what they want?

156. Verifiability. can the requirements be checked?

157. What can tools do for us?

158. What marketing channels do you want to use: e-mail, letter or sms?

159. What if the system wasn t implemented?

160. Validity. does the system provide the functions which best support the customers needs?

161. How does what is being described meet the business need?

162. Basic work/business process; high-level, what is being touched?

163. What happens when requirements are wrong?

164. Completeness. are all functions required by the customer included?

165. Where do system and software requirements come from, what are sources?

166. Consistency. are there any requirements conflicts?

167. Where do you define what is a customer, what are the attributes of customer?

168. Can the requirements be checked?

2.5 Requirements Traceability Matrix: Red Hat OpenShift

169. Why use a WBS?

170. Describe the process for approving requirements so they can be added to the traceability matrix and Red Hat OpenShift project work can be performed. Will the Red Hat OpenShift project requirements become approved in writing?

171. How small is small enough?

172. Do you have a clear understanding of all subcontracts in place?

173. How do you manage scope?

174. Is there a requirements traceability process in place?

175. What is the WBS?

176. How will it affect the stakeholders personally in career?

177. What percentage of Red Hat OpenShift projects are producing traceability matrices between requirements and other work products?

178. Will you use a Requirements Traceability Matrix?

179. Why do you manage scope?

180. What are the chronologies, contingencies, consequences, criteria?

2.6 Project Scope Statement: Red Hat OpenShift

181. Will you need a statement of work?

182. Elements of scope management that deal with concept development ?

183. What are the major deliverables of the Red Hat OpenShift project?

184. Elements that deal with providing the detail?

185. If you were to write a list of what should not be included in the scope statement, what are the things that you would recommend be described as out-of-scope?

186. What process would you recommend for creating the Red Hat OpenShift project scope statement?

187. What is change?

188. Are there completion/verification criteria defined for each task producing an output?

189. Does the scope statement still need some clarity?

190. Is the Red Hat OpenShift project sponsor function identified and defined?

191. Are the input requirements from the team members clearly documented and communicated?

192. Will the qa related information be reported regularly as part of the status reporting mechanisms?

193. Why do you need to manage scope?

194. What are the possible consequences should a risk come to occur?

195. Has the Red Hat OpenShift project scope statement been reviewed as part of the baseline process?

196. Is the plan under configuration management?

197. Is the scope of your Red Hat OpenShift project well defined?

198. Will the risk plan be updated on a regular and frequent basis?

199. Are there specific processes you will use to evaluate and approve/reject changes?

2.7 Assumption and Constraint Log: Red Hat OpenShift

200. Have all involved stakeholders and work groups committed to the Red Hat OpenShift project?

201. Does the system design reflect the requirements?

202. Have the scope, objectives, costs, benefits and impacts been communicated to all involved and/or impacted stakeholders and work groups?

203. How many Red Hat OpenShift project staff does this specific process affect?

204. Contradictory information between document sections?

205. Are there unnecessary steps that are creating bottlenecks and/or causing people to wait?

206. Has a Red Hat OpenShift project Communications Plan been developed?

207. When can log be discarded?

208. What do you audit?

209. Are formal code reviews conducted?

210. How do you design an auditing system?

211. How relevant is this attribute to this Red Hat

OpenShift project or audit?

212. Have you eliminated all duplicative tasks or manual efforts, where appropriate?

213. If appropriate, is the deliverable content consistent with current Red Hat OpenShift project documents and in compliance with the Document Management Plan?

214. Do documented requirements exist for all critical components and areas, including technical, business, interfaces, performance, security and conversion requirements?

215. Have Red Hat OpenShift project management standards and procedures been established and documented?

216. After observing execution of process, is it in compliance with the documented Plan?

217. Is this process still needed?

218. What is positive about the current process?

2.8 Work Breakdown Structure: Red Hat OpenShift

219. Can you make it?

220. How many levels?

221. When do you stop?

222. Who has to do it?

223. Why would you develop a Work Breakdown Structure?

224. Why is it useful?

225. What is the probability that the Red Hat OpenShift project duration will exceed xx weeks?

226. How much detail?

227. Do you need another level?

228. What is the probability of completing the Red Hat OpenShift project in less that xx days?

229. How far down?

230. Where does it take place?

231. How big is a work-package?

232. When does it have to be done?

233. What has to be done?

2.9 WBS Dictionary: Red Hat OpenShift

234. Are direct or indirect cost adjustments being accomplished according to accounting procedures acceptable to us?

235. Does the contractors system provide for accurate cost accumulation and assignment to control accounts in a manner consistent with the budgets using recognized acceptable costing techniques?

236. Are records maintained to show how undistributed budgets are controlled?

237. Changes in the overhead pool and/or organization structures?

238. Software specification, development, integration, and testing, licenses ?

239. Does the contractors system provide unit or lot costs when applicable?

240. Appropriate work authorization documents which subdivide the contractual effort and responsibilities, within functional organizations?

241. Are retroactive changes to budgets for completed work specifically prohibited in an established procedure, and is this procedure adhered to?

242. Does the contractors system include procedures for measuring performance of the lowest level organization responsible for the control account?

243. Are budgets or values assigned to work packages and planning packages in terms of dollars, hours, or other measurable units?

244. Contemplated overhead expenditure for each period based on the best information currently available?

245. Are management actions taken to reduce indirect costs when there are significant adverse variances?

246. Does the scheduling system provide for the identification of work progress against technical and other milestones, and also provide for forecasts of completion dates of scheduled work?

247. Should you have a test for each code module?

248. Are the wbs and organizational levels for application of the Red Hat OpenShift projected overhead costs identified?

249. Are estimates developed by Red Hat OpenShift project personnel coordinated with the already stated responsible for overall management to determine whether required resources will be available according to revised planning?

250. Are retroactive changes to direct costs and indirect costs prohibited except for the correction of errors and routine accounting adjustments?

251. Does the sum of all work package budgets plus planning packages within control accounts equal the budgets assigned to the already stated control accounts?

252. Is the work done on a work package level as described in the WBS dictionary?

2.10 Schedule Management Plan: Red Hat OpenShift

253. Has a Red Hat OpenShift project Communications Plan been developed?

254. Was the scope definition used in task sequencing?

255. Are the processes for schedule assessment and analysis defined?

256. Alignment to strategic goals & objectives?

257. Are internal Red Hat OpenShift project status meetings held at reasonable intervals?

258. Are Red Hat OpenShift project contact logs kept up to date?

259. Are changes in scope (deliverable commitments) agreed to by all affected groups & individuals?

260. Has the ims content been baselined and is it adequately controlled?

261. Are adequate resources provided for the quality assurance function?

262. Is there a set of procedures defining the scope, procedures, and deliverables defining quality control?

263. Are meeting minutes captured and sent out after

the meeting?

264. Is an industry recognized mechanized support tool(s) being used for Red Hat OpenShift project scheduling & tracking?

265. Are risk triggers captured?

266. Are scheduled deliverables actually delivered?

267. Has the schedule been baselined?

268. Have the key functions and capabilities been defined and assigned to each release or iteration?

269. Have key stakeholders been identified?

270. Are the activity durations realistic and at an appropriate level of detail for effective management?

2.11 Activity List: Red Hat OpenShift

271. How difficult will it be to do specific activities on this Red Hat OpenShift project?

272. How should ongoing costs be monitored to try to keep the Red Hat OpenShift project within budget?

273. How detailed should a Red Hat OpenShift project get?

274. The wbs is developed as part of a joint planning session. and how do you know that youhave done this right?

275. What is the LF and LS for each activity?

276. How much slack is available in the Red Hat OpenShift project?

277. When will the work be performed?

278. What did not go as well?

279. When do the individual activities need to start and finish?

280. What are you counting on?

281. How do you determine the late start (LS) for each activity?

282. Should you include sub-activities?

283. How will it be performed?

284. What is the total time required to complete the Red Hat OpenShift project if no delays occur?

285. What will be performed?

286. Are the required resources available or need to be acquired?

287. Is infrastructure setup part of your Red Hat OpenShift project?

288. What is your organizations history in doing similar activities?

289. What is the probability the Red Hat OpenShift project can be completed in xx weeks?

2.12 Activity Attributes: Red Hat OpenShift

290. Why?

291. Resources to accomplish the work?

292. How much activity detail is required?

293. What went wrong?

294. How else could the items be grouped?

295. Can more resources be added?

296. How many resources do you need to complete the work scope within a limit of X number of days?

297. Are the required resources available?

298. How difficult will it be to do specific activities on this Red Hat OpenShift project?

299. Were there other ways you could have organized the data to achieve similar results?

300. Have constraints been applied to the start and finish milestones for the phases?

301. Activity: what is In the Bag?

302. What activity do you think you should spend the most time on?

303. Is there a trend during the year?

304. Have you identified the Activity Leveling Priority code value on each activity?

305. What is missing?

2.13 Milestone List: Red Hat OpenShift

306. Competitive advantages?

307. Milestone pages should display the UserID of the person who added the milestone. Does a report or query exist that provides this audit information?

308. Sustainable financial backing?

309. How difficult will it be to do specific activities on this Red Hat OpenShift project?

310. How soon can the activity finish?

311. Which path is the critical path?

312. What specific improvements did you make to the Red Hat OpenShift project proposal since the previous time?

313. How will you get the word out to customers?

314. Can you derive how soon can the whole Red Hat OpenShift project finish?

315. How soon can the activity start?

316. What is the market for your technology, product or service?

317. How will the milestone be verified?

318. How do you manage time?

319. How late can each activity be finished and started?

320. When will the Red Hat OpenShift project be complete?

321. What date will the task finish?

322. Global influences?

323. Information and research?

2.14 Network Diagram: Red Hat OpenShift

324. What job or jobs could run concurrently?

325. What activities must follow this activity?

326. Where do you schedule uncertainty time?

327. How confident can you be in your milestone dates and the delivery date?

328. What are the Key Success Factors?

329. Can you calculate the confidence level?

330. Which type of network diagram allows you to depict four types of dependencies?

331. What are the Major Administrative Issues?

332. If the Red Hat OpenShift project network diagram cannot change and you have extra personnel resources, what is the BEST thing to do?

333. What is the lowest cost to complete this Red Hat OpenShift project in xx weeks?

334. What controls the start and finish of a job?

335. Why must you schedule milestones, such as reviews, throughout the Red Hat OpenShift project?

336. What is the probability of completing the Red Hat OpenShift project in less that xx days?

337. If a current contract exists, can you provide the vendor name, contract start, and contract expiration date?

338. Where do schedules come from?

339. What is the completion time?

340. What activity must be completed immediately before this activity can start?

341. Are the gantt chart and/or network diagram updated periodically and used to assess the overall Red Hat OpenShift project timetable?

2.15 Activity Resource Requirements: Red Hat OpenShift

342. Are there unresolved issues that need to be addressed?

343. Which logical relationship does the PDM use most often?

344. How many signatures do you require on a check and does this match what is in your policy and procedures?

345. Is there anything planned that does not need to be here?

346. Why do you do that?

347. What are constraints that you might find during the Human Resource Planning process?

348. What is the Work Plan Standard?

349. Anything else?

350. When does monitoring begin?

351. Organizational Applicability?

352. Other support in specific areas?

353. Do you use tools like decomposition and rolling-wave planning to produce the activity list and other

outputs?

354. Time for overtime?

355. How do you handle petty cash?

2.16 Resource Breakdown Structure: Red Hat OpenShift

356. How difficult will it be to do specific activities on this Red Hat OpenShift project?

357. How can this help you with team building?

358. What is each stakeholders desired outcome for the Red Hat OpenShift project?

359. The list could probably go on, but, the thing that you would most like to know is, How long & How much?

360. Is predictive resource analysis being done?

361. Goals for the Red Hat OpenShift project. What is each stakeholders desired outcome for the Red Hat OpenShift project?

362. Why do you do it?

363. Who will use the system?

364. What is the difference between % Complete and % work?

365. What is the purpose of assigning and documenting responsibility?

366. Which resource planning tool provides information on resource responsibility and

accountability?

367. Who needs what information?

368. What defines a successful Red Hat OpenShift project?

369. What can you do to improve productivity?

370. What defines a successful Red Hat OpenShift project?

371. Who is allowed to perform which functions?

372. What is Red Hat OpenShift project communication management?

373. How should the information be delivered?

374. Who delivers the information?

2.17 Activity Duration Estimates: Red Hat OpenShift

375. What is the BEST thing to do?

376. Is a work breakdown structure created to organize and to confirm the scope of each Red Hat OpenShift project?

377. How difficult will it be to do specific activities on this Red Hat OpenShift project?

378. What are the ways to create and distribute Red Hat OpenShift project performance information?

379. List five reasons why organizations outsource. Why is there a growing trend in outsourcing, especially in the government?

380. Why do you think schedule issues often cause the most conflicts on Red Hat OpenShift projects?

381. Do an internet search on earning pmp certification. be sure to search for yahoo groups related to this topic. what are the options you found to help people prepare for the exam?

382. Total slack can be calculated by which equations?

383. Why is there a new or renewed interest in the field of Red Hat OpenShift project management?

384. Are Red Hat OpenShift project records organized,

maintained, and assessable by Red Hat OpenShift project team members?

385. Is evaluation criteria defined to rate proposals?

386. What is the critical path for this Red Hat OpenShift project and how long is it?

387. Do scope statements include the Red Hat OpenShift project objectives and expected deliverables?

388. Does a process exist to identify Red Hat OpenShift project roles, responsibilities and reporting relationships?

389. Describe a Red Hat OpenShift project that suffered from scope creep. Could it have been avoided?

390. Is the Red Hat OpenShift project performing better or worse than planned?

391. How difficult will it be to complete specific activities on this Red Hat OpenShift project?

392. Is a formal written notice that the contract is complete provided to the seller?

393. What tasks must follow this task?

394. Calculate the expected duration for an activity that has a most likely time of 3, a pessimistic time of 10, and a optimiztic time of 2?

2.18 Duration Estimating Worksheet: Red Hat OpenShift

395. Is a construction detail attached (to aid in explanation)?

396. What utility impacts are there?

397. Do any colleagues have experience with your organization and/or RFPs?

398. For other activities, how much delay can be tolerated?

399. What is the total time required to complete the Red Hat OpenShift project if no delays occur?

400. How can the Red Hat OpenShift project be displayed graphically to better visualize the activities?

401. What questions do you have?

402. Why estimate time and cost?

403. What is an Average Red Hat OpenShift project?

404. What work will be included in the Red Hat OpenShift project?

405. Will the Red Hat OpenShift project collaborate with the local community and leverage resources?

406. What is cost and Red Hat OpenShift project cost

management?

407. Why estimate costs?

408. What is your role?

409. Science = process: remember the scientific method?

410. Is this operation cost effective?

411. Can the Red Hat OpenShift project be constructed as planned?

412. Define the work as completely as possible. What work will be included in the Red Hat OpenShift project?

2.19 Project Schedule: Red Hat OpenShift

413. How can you fix it?

414. Why or why not?

415. Are procedures defined by which the Red Hat OpenShift project schedule may be changed?

416. How do you manage Red Hat OpenShift project Risk?

417. What documents, if any, will the subcontractor provide (eg Red Hat OpenShift project schedule, quality plan etc)?

418. Verify that the update is accurate. Are all remaining durations correct?

419. Are key risk mitigation strategies added to the Red Hat OpenShift project schedule?

420. Does the condition or event threaten the Red Hat OpenShift projects objectives in any ways?

421. Is there a Schedule Management Plan that establishes the criteria and activities for developing, monitoring and controlling the Red Hat OpenShift project schedule?

422. It allows the Red Hat OpenShift project to be delivered on schedule. How Do you Use Schedules?

423. Are all remaining durations correct?

424. How can you minimize or control changes to Red Hat OpenShift project schedules?

425. Is the structure for tracking the Red Hat OpenShift project schedule well defined and assigned to a specific individual?

426. Schedule/cost recovery?

427. Is the Red Hat OpenShift project schedule available for all Red Hat OpenShift project team members to review?

428. How detailed should a Red Hat OpenShift project get?

429. How effectively were issues able to be resolved without impacting the Red Hat OpenShift project Schedule or Budget?

430. Month Red Hat OpenShift project take?

2.20 Cost Management Plan: Red Hat OpenShift

431. Is there an approved case?

432. Change types and category – What are the types of changes and what are the techniques to report and control changes?

433. Is there a Steering Committee in place?

434. Will the earned value reporting interface between time and cost management?

435. Were Red Hat OpenShift project team members involved in the development of activity & task decomposition?

436. Is documentation created for communication with the suppliers and Vendors?

437. Is there a formal set of procedures supporting Stakeholder Management?

438. Are action items captured and managed?

439. Is stakeholder involvement adequate?

440. What is an Acceptance Management Process?

441. Weve met your goals?

442. Does the Red Hat OpenShift project have a

formal Red Hat OpenShift project Charter?

443. Is current scope of the Red Hat OpenShift project substantially different than that originally defined?

444. Does the business case include how the Red Hat OpenShift project aligns with your organizations strategic goals & objectives?

445. Are risk oriented checklists used during risk identification?

446. Is your organization certified as a broker of the products/supplies?

447. Have the key elements of a coherent Red Hat OpenShift project management strategy been established?

448. Scope of work – What is the likelihood and extent of potential future changes to the Red Hat OpenShift project scope?

449. Best practices implementation – How will change management be applied to this Red Hat OpenShift project?

450. What is Red Hat OpenShift project cost management?

2.21 Activity Cost Estimates: Red Hat OpenShift

451. Does the estimator estimate by task or by person?

452. What is included in indirect cost being allocated?

453. Certification of actual expenditures?

454. How do you change activities?

455. Can you change your activities?

456. What were things that you need to improve?

457. How do you fund change orders?

458. Were escalated issues resolved promptly?

459. Is costing method consistent with study goals?

460. Was it performed on time?

461. What cost data should be used to estimate costs during the 2-year follow-up period?

462. What are the audit requirements?

463. What makes a good activity description?

464. Where can you get activity reports?

465. How difficult will it be to do specific tasks on the Red Hat OpenShift project?

2.22 Cost Estimating Worksheet: Red Hat OpenShift

466. Identify the timeframe necessary to monitor progress and collect data to determine how the selected measure has changed?

467. What is the estimated labor cost today based upon this information?

468. What info is needed?

469. What costs are to be estimated?

470. Is the Red Hat OpenShift project responsive to community need?

471. Value pocket identification & quantification what are value pockets?

472. Can a trend be established from historical performance data on the selected measure and are the criteria for using trend analysis or forecasting methods met?

473. Will the Red Hat OpenShift project collaborate with the local community and leverage resources?

474. What will others want?

475. What happens to any remaining funds not used?

476. Who is best positioned to know and assist in

identifying corresponding factors?

477. How will the results be shared and to whom?

478. What can be included?

479. Ask: are others positioned to know, are others credible, and will others cooperate?

480. Does the Red Hat OpenShift project provide innovative ways for stakeholders to overcome obstacles or deliver better outcomes?

481. Is it feasible to establish a control group arrangement?

482. What additional Red Hat OpenShift project(s) could be initiated as a result of this Red Hat OpenShift project?

483. What is the purpose of estimating?

2.23 Cost Baseline: Red Hat OpenShift

484. Has training and knowledge transfer of the operations organization been completed?

485. How likely is it to go wrong?

486. What is the reality?

487. Has the Red Hat OpenShift project documentation been archived or otherwise disposed as described in the Red Hat OpenShift project communication plan?

488. Are there contingencies or conditions related to the acceptance?

489. What is cost and Red Hat OpenShift project cost management?

490. Who will use corresponding metrics ?

491. How do you manage cost?

492. Is the requested change request a result of changes in other Red Hat OpenShift project(s)?

493. Why do you manage cost?

494. Is request in line with priorities?

495. Where do changes come from?

496. Has the Red Hat OpenShift projected annual cost

to operate and maintain the product(s) or service(s) been approved and funded?

497. Vac -variance at completion, how much over/ under budget do you expect to be?

498. What can go wrong?

499. Are you meeting with your team regularly?

500. Have you identified skills that are missing from your team?

501. For what purpose ?

502. What is your organizations history in doing similar tasks?

503. Have the resources used by the Red Hat OpenShift project been reassigned to other units or Red Hat OpenShift projects?

2.24 Quality Management Plan: Red Hat OpenShift

504. How relevant is this attribute to this Red Hat OpenShift project or audit?

505. When reporting to different audiences, do you vary the form or type of report?

506. Are there processes in place to ensure internal consistency between the source code components?

507. Has a Red Hat OpenShift project Communications Plan been developed?

508. Are you meeting the quality standards?

509. How are calibration records kept?

510. Methodology followed?

511. What would you gain if you spent time working to improve this process?

512. Was trending evident between reviews?

513. What process do you use to minimize errors, defects, and rework?

514. Are qmps good forever?

515. How does the material compare to a regulatory threshold?

516. How do senior leaders review organizational performance?

517. What has the QM Collaboration done?

518. Is there a Quality Management Plan?

519. What is your organizations strategic planning process?

520. Can it be done better?

521. Have all involved stakeholders and work groups committed to the Red Hat OpenShift project?

522. What are you trying to accomplish?

523. How does your organization ensure the quality, reliability, and user-friendliness of its hardware and software?

2.25 Quality Metrics: Red Hat OpenShift

524. How do you calculate such metrics?

525. Are applicable standards referenced and available?

526. What level of statistical confidence do you use?

527. Is there alignment within your organization on definitions?

528. How are requirements conflicts resolved?

529. Have risk areas been identified?

530. Has risk analysis been adequately reviewed?

531. What are your organizations next steps?

532. Filter visualizations of interest?

533. Has trace of defects been initiated?

534. What approved evidence based screening tools can be used?

535. Has it met internal or external standards?

536. How do you communicate results and findings to upper management?

537. Are quality metrics defined?

538. When is the security analysis testing complete?

539. How is it being measured?

540. What documentation is required?

541. Are there any open risk issues?

542. What method of measurement do you use?

2.26 Process Improvement Plan: Red Hat OpenShift

543. Who should prepare the process improvement action plan?

544. Where do you want to be?

545. Management commitment at all levels?

546. Has a process guide to collect the data been developed?

547. Everyone agrees on what process improvement is, right?

548. Have the frequency of collection and the points in the process where measurements will be made been determined?

549. Have the supporting tools been developed or acquired?

550. Modeling current processes is great, and will you ever see a return on that investment?

551. Are you making progress on your improvement plan?

552. Are you following the quality standards?

553. What lessons have you learned so far?

554. If a process improvement framework is being used, which elements will help the problems and goals listed?

555. Are there forms and procedures to collect and record the data?

556. Where do you focus?

557. Does explicit definition of the measures exist?

558. What makes people good SPI coaches?

559. The motive is determined by asking, Why do you want to achieve this goal?

560. What personnel are the change agents for your initiative?

561. How do you manage quality?

2.27 Responsibility Assignment Matrix: Red Hat OpenShift

562. Are the bases and rates for allocating costs from each indirect pool consistently applied?

563. Which Red Hat OpenShift project management knowledge area is least mature?

564. With too many people labeled as doing the work, are there too many hands involved?

565. Will too many Communicating responsibilities tangle the Red Hat OpenShift project in unnecessary communications?

566. Does each activity-deliverable have exactly one Accountable responsibility, so that accountability is clear and decisions can be made quickly?

567. Is the entire contract planned in time-phased control accounts to the extent practicable?

568. Are all authorized tasks assigned to identified organizational elements?

569. Changes in the nature of the overhead requirements?

570. How cost benefit analysis?

571. Are material costs reported within the same period as that in which BCWP is earned for that

material?

572. What do you need to implement earned value management?

573. Are the wbs and organizational levels for application of the Red Hat OpenShift projected overhead costs identified?

574. What is the justification?

575. Budgets assigned to control accounts?

576. Do others have the time to dedicate to your Red Hat OpenShift project?

577. The already stated responsible for overhead performance control of related costs?

578. How many people do you need?

579. Do work packages consist of discrete tasks which are adequately described?

2.28 Roles and Responsibilities: Red Hat OpenShift

580. Concern: where are you limited or have no authority, where you can not influence?

581. What expectations were NOT met?

582. Key conclusions and recommendations: Are conclusions and recommendations relevant and acceptable?

583. Influence: what areas of organizational decision making are you able to influence when you do not have authority to make the final decision?

584. What are your major roles and responsibilities in the area of performance measurement and assessment?

585. Accountabilities: what are the roles and responsibilities of individual team members?

586. What expectations were met?

587. What should you do now to ensure that you are exceeding expectations and excelling in your current position?

588. Who is responsible for implementation activities and where will the functions, roles and responsibilities be defined?

589. Required skills, knowledge, experience?

590. What should you do now to ensure that you are meeting all expectations of your current position?

591. Is the data complete?

592. Was the expectation clearly communicated?

593. Who is involved?

594. Be specific; avoid generalities. Thank you and great work alone are insufficient. What exactly do you appreciate and why?

595. Once the responsibilities are defined for the Red Hat OpenShift project, have the deliverables, roles and responsibilities been clearly communicated to every participant?

596. Do the values and practices inherent in the culture of your organization foster or hinder the process?

597. Does your vision/mission support a culture of quality data?

598. What specific behaviors did you observe?

2.29 Human Resource Management Plan: Red Hat OpenShift

599. Have adequate resources been provided by management to ensure Red Hat OpenShift project success?

600. Have Red Hat OpenShift project success criteria been defined?

601. Are changes in deliverable commitments agreed to by all affected groups & individuals?

602. Identify who is needed on the core Red Hat OpenShift project team to complete Red Hat OpenShift project deliverables and achieve its goals and objectives. What skills, knowledge and experiences are required?

603. How are you going to ensure that you have a well motivated workforce?

604. What areas were overlooked on this Red Hat OpenShift project?

605. Is your organization primarily focused on a specific industry?

606. Are decisions captured in a decisions log?

607. Are enough systems & user personnel assigned to the Red Hat OpenShift project?

608. Personnel with expertise?

609. Is this Red Hat OpenShift project carried out in partnership with other groups/organizations?

610. Is the schedule updated on a periodic basis?

611. Quality assurance overheads?

612. Are corrective actions and variances reported?

613. Has a structured approach been used to break work effort into manageable components (WBS)?

614. Are the schedule estimates reasonable given the Red Hat OpenShift project?

2.30 Communications Management Plan: Red Hat OpenShift

615. What is the stakeholders level of authority?

616. How do you manage communications?

617. Who are the members of the governing body?

618. Are others needed?

619. How often do you engage with stakeholders?

620. How did the term stakeholder originate?

621. Who is the stakeholder?

622. Do you ask; can you recommend others for you to talk with about this initiative?

623. Which stakeholders can influence others?

624. Where do team members get information?

625. Can you think of other people who might have concerns or interests?

626. Who will use or be affected by the result of a Red Hat OpenShift project?

627. Is there an important stakeholder who is actively opposed and will not receive messages?

628. Are you constantly rushing from meeting to meeting?

629. Who to share with?

630. Why do you manage communications?

631. What steps can you take for a positive relationship?

632. Are there potential barriers between the team and the stakeholder?

633. Are others part of the communications management plan?

634. Are the stakeholders getting the information others need, are others consulted, are concerns addressed?

2.31 Risk Management Plan: Red Hat OpenShift

635. Which risks should get the attention?

636. Do end-users have realistic expectations?

637. Costs associated with late delivery or a defective product?

638. What is the probability the risk avoidance strategy will be successful?

639. How are risk analysis and prioritization performed?

640. Financial risk -can your organization afford to undertake the Red Hat OpenShift project?

641. Was an original risk assessment/risk management plan completed?

642. Is the necessary data being captured and is it complete and accurate?

643. Is the number of people on the Red Hat OpenShift project team adequate to do the job?

644. Should the risk be taken at all?

645. How do you manage Red Hat OpenShift project Risk?

646. Is there anything you would now do differently on your Red Hat OpenShift project based on this experience?

647. Do requirements demand the use of new analysis, design, or testing methods?

648. Management -what contingency plans do you have if the risk becomes a reality?

649. Technology risk: is the Red Hat OpenShift project technically feasible?

650. How is the audit profession changing?

651. What does a risk management program do?

652. Who/what can assist?

653. Market risk -will the new service or product be useful to your organization or marketable to others?

654. How will the Red Hat OpenShift project know if your organizations risk response actions were effective?

2.32 Risk Register: Red Hat OpenShift

655. What should you do now?

656. Are your objectives at risk?

657. What are the main aims, objectives of the policy, strategy, or service and the intended outcomes?

658. Are there any knock-on effects/impact on any of the other areas?

659. Cost/benefit – how much will the proposed mitigations cost and how does this cost compare with the potential cost of the risk event/situation should it occur?

660. What is the probability and impact of the risk occurring?

661. Risk categories: what are the main categories of risks that should be addressed on this Red Hat OpenShift project?

662. What are your key risks/show istoppers and what is being done to manage them?

663. Does the evidence highlight any areas to advance opportunities or foster good relations. If yes what steps will be taken?

664. Schedule impact/severity estimated range (workdays) assume the event happens, what is the potential impact?

665. What has changed since the last period?

666. What can be done about it?

667. Which key risks have ineffective responses or outstanding improvement actions?

668. What is a Community Risk Register?

669. When will it happen?

670. What could prevent you delivering on the strategic program objectives and what is being done to mitigate corresponding issues?

671. How are risks graded?

672. Are corrective measures implemented as planned?

673. What should the audit role be in establishing a risk management process?

674. Contingency actions - planned actions to reduce the immediate seriousness of the risk when it does occur. What should you do when?

2.33 Probability and Impact Assessment: Red Hat OpenShift

675. Does the software interface with new or unproven hardware or unproven vendor products?

676. Who are the international/overseas Red Hat OpenShift project partners (equipment supplier/supplier/consultant/contractor) for this Red Hat OpenShift project?

677. What is the experience (performance, attitude, business ethics, etc.) in the past with contractors?

678. What things are likely to change?

679. Who has experience with this?

680. Are staff committed for the duration of the Red Hat OpenShift project?

681. Is the customer willing to establish rapid communication links with the developer?

682. Is the number of people on the Red Hat OpenShift project team adequate to do the job?

683. What are the channels available for distribution to the customer?

684. Is a software Red Hat OpenShift project management tool available?

685. How is the risk management process used in practice?

686. What significant shift will occur in governmental policies, laws, and regulations pertaining to specific industries?

687. Do you manage the process through use of metrics?

688. How realistic is the timing of introduction?

689. What are the chances the risk event will occur?

690. How do you maximize short-term return on investment?

691. Do you have a consistent repeatable process that is actually used?

692. How do risks change during a Red Hat OpenShift project life cycle?

693. What will be cost of redeployment of personnel?

694. Risk may be made during which step of risk management?

2.34 Probability and Impact Matrix: Red Hat OpenShift

695. Are formal technical reviews part of this process?

696. How would you assess the risk management process in the Red Hat OpenShift project?

697. How would you define a risk?

698. Premium on reliability of product?

699. Risk categorization -which of your categories has more risk than others?

700. How do you analyze the risks in the different types of Red Hat OpenShift projects?

701. Which risks need to move on to Perform Quantitative Risk Analysis?

702. How carefully have the potential competitors been identified?

703. How well is the risk understood?

704. Are you on schedule?

705. Do you train all developers in the process?

706. Degree of confidence in estimated size estimate?

707. Which phase of the Red Hat OpenShift project do

you take part in?

708. How are risks and risk management perceived in the Red Hat OpenShift project?

709. How do risks change during the Red Hat OpenShift projects life cycle?

710. Is the present organizational structure for handling the Red Hat OpenShift project sufficient?

711. Are tools for analysis and design available?

712. What has the Red Hat OpenShift project manager forgotten to do?

713. What will be the likely incidence of conflict with neighboring Red Hat OpenShift projects?

2.35 Risk Data Sheet: Red Hat OpenShift

714. How can it happen?

715. During work activities could hazards exist?

716. Has the most cost-effective solution been chosen?

717. What are the main opportunities available to you that you should grab while you can?

718. What do you know?

719. How do you handle product safely?

720. What are you trying to achieve (Objectives)?

721. What are you weak at and therefore need to do better?

722. What are the main threats to your existence?

723. What can happen?

724. What is the environment within which you operate (social trends, economic, community values, broad based participation, national directions etc.)?

725. Potential for recurrence?

726. How can hazards be reduced?

727. What actions can be taken to eliminate or remove risk?

728. What are your core values?

729. What can you do?

730. What will be the consequences if the risk happens?

731. Whom do you serve (customers)?

732. How reliable is the data source?

733. What was measured?

2.36 Procurement Management Plan: Red Hat OpenShift

734. Do all stakeholders know how to access the PM repository and where to find the Red Hat OpenShift project documentation?

735. Financial capacity; does the seller have, or can the seller reasonably be expected to obtain, the financial resources needed?

736. Are the results of quality assurance reviews provided to affected groups & individuals?

737. Is the Red Hat OpenShift project sponsor clearly communicating the business case or rationale for why this Red Hat OpenShift project is needed?

738. If independent estimates will be needed as evaluation criteria, who will prepare them and when?

739. Is there an on-going process in place to monitor Red Hat OpenShift project risks?

740. Were Red Hat OpenShift project team members involved in the development of activity & task decomposition?

741. Is the structure for tracking the Red Hat OpenShift project schedule well defined and assigned to a specific individual?

742. Is it standard practice to formally commit

stakeholders to the Red Hat OpenShift project via agreements?

743. Are the schedule estimates reasonable given the Red Hat OpenShift project?

744. Are key risk mitigation strategies added to the Red Hat OpenShift project schedule?

745. Are trade-offs between accepting the risk and mitigating the risk identified?

746. Is there a formal set of procedures supporting Issues Management?

747. Are target dates established for each milestone deliverable?

748. Are change requests logged and managed?

749. Are the payment terms being followed?

750. Public engagement – did you get it right?

751. Is pert / critical path or equivalent methodology being used?

2.37 Source Selection Criteria: Red Hat OpenShift

752. What documentation should be used to support the selection decision?

753. Can you prevent comparison of proposals?

754. Is experience evaluated?

755. Are considerations anticipated?

756. What benefits are accrued from issuing a DRFP in advance of issuing a final RFP?

757. How much past performance information should be requested?

758. What are the most common types of rating systems?

759. What is price analysis and when should it be performed?

760. How organization are proposed quotes/prices?

761. Is there collaboration among your evaluators?

762. What documentation is needed for a tradeoff decision?

763. Are they compliant with all technical requirements?

764. Comparison of each offers prices to the estimated prices -are there significant differences?

765. How will you decide an evaluators write up is sufficient?

766. Does your documentation identify why the team concurs or differs with reported performance from past performance report (CPARs, questionnaire responses, etc.)?

767. What common questions or problems are associated with debriefings?

768. How do you facilitate evaluation against published criteria?

769. What should be the contracting officers strategy?

770. What are the guidelines regarding award without considerations?

771. In which phase of the acquisition process cycle does source qualifications reside?

2.38 Stakeholder Management Plan: Red Hat OpenShift

772. Are regulatory inspections considered part of quality control?

773. Are Red Hat OpenShift project team members involved in detailed estimating and scheduling?

774. Have Red Hat OpenShift project management standards and procedures been identified / established and documented?

775. Where does the information come from?

776. What information should be collected?

777. Who might be involved in developing a charter?

778. Have Red Hat OpenShift project success criteria been defined?

779. Is staff trained on the software technologies that are being used on the Red Hat OpenShift project?

780. What other teams / processes would be impacted by changes to the current process, and how?

781. Have process improvement efforts been completed before requirements efforts begin?

782. What is meant by managing the triple constraint?

783. Are vendor invoices audited for accuracy before payment?

784. Is a stakeholder management plan in place?

785. What is to be the method of release?

786. Detail warranty and/or maintenance periods?

787. What sources of information are reliable?

2.39 Change Management Plan: Red Hat OpenShift

788. What will be the preferred method of delivery?

789. Who should be involved in developing a change management strategy?

790. What provokes organizational change?

791. What risks may occur upfront?

792. What are the key change management success metrics?

793. Where will the funds come from?

794. What prerequisite knowledge or training is required?

795. What new roles are needed?

796. Is it the same for each of the business units?

797. Is there support for this application(s) and are the details available for distribution?

798. What is the worst thing that can happen if you chose not to communicate this information?

799. Do the proposed users have access to the appropriate documentation?

800. What is the most cynical response it can receive?

801. How will the stakeholders share information and transfer knowledge?

802. How do you know the requirements you documented are the right ones?

803. Is there a support model for this application and are the details available for distribution?

804. Has the target training audience been identified and nominated?

805. How far reaching in your organization is the change?

806. When to start change management?

807. What is the most positive interpretation it can receive?

3.0 Executing Process Group: Red Hat OpenShift

808. What were things that you did very well and want to do the same again on the next Red Hat OpenShift project?

809. Will outside resources be needed to help?

810. What are some crucial elements of a good Red Hat OpenShift project plan?

811. Would you rate yourself as being risk-averse, risk-neutral, or risk-seeking?

812. It under budget or over budget?

813. Who will provide training?

814. Is the Red Hat OpenShift project performing better or worse than planned?

815. How well did the team follow the chosen processes?

816. How can your organization use a weighted decision matrix to evaluate proposals as part of source selection?

817. Do your results resemble a normal distribution?

818. What are the critical steps involved with strategy mapping?

819. Why should Red Hat OpenShift project managers strive to make jobs look easy?

820. What type of people would you want on your team?

821. What are the challenges Red Hat OpenShift project teams face?

822. How is Red Hat OpenShift project performance information created and distributed?

823. Who are the Red Hat OpenShift project stakeholders?

824. How could you control progress of your Red Hat OpenShift project?

3.1 Team Member Status Report: Red Hat OpenShift

825. Are your organizations Red Hat OpenShift projects more successful over time?

826. Will the staff do training or is that done by a third party?

827. How it is to be done?

828. How does this product, good, or service meet the needs of the Red Hat OpenShift project and your organization as a whole?

829. Is there evidence that staff is taking a more professional approach toward management of your organizations Red Hat OpenShift projects?

830. Are the products of your organizations Red Hat OpenShift projects meeting customers objectives?

831. What specific interest groups do you have in place?

832. Why is it to be done?

833. How much risk is involved?

834. The problem with Reward & Recognition Programs is that the truly deserving people all too often get left out. How can you make it practical?

835. Does every department have to have a Red Hat OpenShift project Manager on staff?

836. Are the attitudes of staff regarding Red Hat OpenShift project work improving?

837. What is to be done?

838. Do you have an Enterprise Red Hat OpenShift project Management Office (EPMO)?

839. Does the product, good, or service already exist within your organization?

840. When a teams productivity and success depend on collaboration and the efficient flow of information, what generally fails them?

841. How will resource planning be done?

842. How can you make it practical?

843. Does your organization have the means (staff, money, contract, etc.) to produce or to acquire the product, good, or service?

3.2 Change Request: Red Hat OpenShift

844. Has a formal technical review been conducted to assess technical correctness?

845. What is the function of the change control committee?

846. What are the requirements for urgent changes?

847. Will all change requests be unconditionally tracked through this process?

848. What type of changes does change control take into account?

849. When do you create a change request?

850. How are changes graded and who is responsible for the rating?

851. Can you answer what happened, who did it, when did it happen, and what else will be affected?

852. Who can suggest changes?

853. Who is responsible for the implementation and monitoring of all measures?

854. Will this change conflict with other requirements changes (e.g., lead to conflicting operational scenarios)?

855. Are there requirements attributes that can discriminate between high and low reliability?

856. How is the change documented (format, content, storage)?

857. Does the schedule include Red Hat OpenShift project management time and change request analysis time?

858. What can be filed?

859. Has your address changed?

860. What must be taken into consideration when introducing change control programs?

861. Who is included in the change control team?

862. Will all change requests and current status be logged?

863. What is the change request log?

3.3 Change Log: Red Hat OpenShift

864. How does this change affect the timeline of the schedule?

865. Does the suggested change request seem to represent a necessary enhancement to the product?

866. Is the change request within Red Hat OpenShift project scope?

867. When was the request approved?

868. Is the requested change request a result of changes in other Red Hat OpenShift project(s)?

869. How does this change affect scope?

870. Is this a mandatory replacement?

871. Should a more thorough impact analysis be conducted?

872. Does the suggested change request represent a desired enhancement to the products functionality?

873. When was the request submitted?

874. Do the described changes impact on the integrity or security of the system?

875. Will the Red Hat OpenShift project fail if the change request is not executed?

876. Is the change request open, closed or pending?

877. Is the submitted change a new change or a modification of a previously approved change?

878. Is the change backward compatible without limitations?

879. How does this relate to the standards developed for specific business processes?

880. Who initiated the change request?

3.4 Decision Log: Red Hat OpenShift

881. Linked to original objective?

882. Who is the decisionmaker?

883. Meeting purpose; why does this team meet?

884. What are the cost implications?

885. Is your opponent open to a non-traditional workflow, or will it likely challenge anything you do?

886. How does the use a Decision Support System influence the strategies/tactics or costs?

887. At what point in time does loss become unacceptable?

888. How consolidated and comprehensive a story can you tell by capturing currently available incident data in a central location and through a log of key decisions during an incident?

889. What is the average size of your matters in an applicable measurement?

890. What was the rationale for the decision?

891. How do you define success?

892. Behaviors; what are guidelines that the team has identified that will assist them with getting the most out of team meetings?

893. What is the line where eDiscovery ends and document review begins?

894. Who will be given a copy of this document and where will it be kept?

895. Adversarial environment. is your opponent open to a non-traditional workflow, or will it likely challenge anything you do?

896. Which variables make a critical difference?

897. How does provision of information, both in terms of content and presentation, influence acceptance of alternative strategies?

898. How effective is maintaining the log at facilitating organizational learning?

899. What is your overall strategy for quality control / quality assurance procedures?

900. What eDiscovery problem or issue did your organization set out to fix or make better?

3.5 Quality Audit: Red Hat OpenShift

901. What does an analysis of your organizations staff profile suggest in terms of its planning, and how is this being addressed?

902. How does your organization know that its system for ensuring that its training activities are appropriately resourced and support is appropriately effective and constructive?

903. How does your organization know that its staff embody the core knowledge, skills and characteristics for which it wishes to be recognized?

904. Does the audit organization have experience in performing the required work for entities of your type and size?

905. How does your organization know that its methods are appropriately effective and constructive?

906. What are your supplier audits?

907. How does your organization know that its research funding systems are appropriately effective and constructive in enabling quality research outcomes?

908. How does your organization know that its system for recruiting the best staff possible are appropriately effective and constructive?

909. How does your organization know that it

provides a safe and healthy environment?

910. Does the suppliers quality system have a written procedure for corrective action when a defect occurs?

911. How does your organization know that its relationships with industry and employers are appropriately effective and constructive?

912. How does your organization know that it is effectively and constructively guiding staff through to timely completion of tasks?

913. How does your organization know that its promotions system is appropriately effective, constructive and fair?

914. How well do you think your organization engages with the outside community?

915. For each device to be reconditioned, are device specifications, such as appropriate engineering drawings, component specifications and software specifications, maintained?

916. Are all staff empowered and encouraged to contribute to ongoing improvement efforts?

917. How does your organization know that its staff placements are appropriately effective and constructive in relation to program-related learning outcomes?

918. What happens if your organization fails its Quality Audit?

919. How are you auditing your organizations compliance with regulations?

920. How does your organization know that its processes for managing severance are appropriately effective, constructive and fair?

3.6 Team Directory: Red Hat OpenShift

921. Process decisions: do invoice amounts match accepted work in place?

922. Who will write the meeting minutes and distribute?

923. Days from the time the issue is identified?

924. Who will report Red Hat OpenShift project status to all stakeholders?

925. Decisions: is the most suitable form of contract being used?

926. Who will talk to the customer?

927. How will you accomplish and manage the objectives?

928. Who will be the stakeholders on your next Red Hat OpenShift project?

929. Process decisions: are there any statutory or regulatory issues relevant to the timely execution of work?

930. Process decisions: do job conditions warrant additional actions to collect job information and document on-site activity?

931. Have you decided when to celebrate the Red Hat OpenShift projects completion date?

932. Decisions: what could be done better to improve the quality of the constructed product?

933. When does information need to be distributed?

934. How do unidentified risks impact the outcome of the Red Hat OpenShift project?

935. Process decisions: how well was task order work performed?

936. Contract requirements complied with?

937. Who is the Sponsor?

938. Is construction on schedule?

939. Who are the Team Members?

3.7 Team Operating Agreement: Red Hat OpenShift

940. Why does your organization want to participate in teaming?

941. Do you prevent individuals from dominating the meeting?

942. What is culture?

943. Do you call or email participants to ensure understanding, follow-through and commitment to the meeting outcomes?

944. To whom do you deliver your services?

945. How will you divide work equitably?

946. Are there more than two national cultures represented by your team?

947. Do team members need to frequently communicate as a full group to make timely decisions?

948. What is the anticipated procedure (recruitment, solicitation of volunteers, or assignment) for selecting team members?

949. Did you prepare participants for the next meeting?

950. Do you leverage technology engagement tools group chat, polls, screen sharing, etc.?

951. Have you established procedures that team members can follow to work effectively together, such as a team operating agreement?

952. What types of accommodations will be formulated and put in place for sustaining the team?

953. Must your members collaborate successfully to complete Red Hat OpenShift projects?

954. How will your group handle planned absences?

955. What is a Virtual Team?

956. What are the current caseload numbers in the unit?

957. Is compensation based on team and individual performance?

958. Are there differences in access to communication and collaboration technology based on team member location?

3.8 Team Performance Assessment: Red Hat OpenShift

959. How does Red Hat OpenShift project termination impact Red Hat OpenShift project team members?

960. To what degree can the team measure progress against specific goals?

961. To what degree are the skill areas critical to team performance present?

962. To what degree will new and supplemental skills be introduced as the need is recognized?

963. To what degree do team members understand one anothers roles and skills?

964. Individual task proficiency and team process behavior: what is important for team functioning?

965. To what degree are the relative importance and priority of the goals clear to all team members?

966. To what degree can team members meet frequently enough to accomplish the teams ends?

967. To what degree can team members vigorously define the teams purpose in considerations with others who are not part of the functioning team?

968. To what degree do team members frequently explore the teams purpose and its implications?

969. Do you give group members authority to make at least some important decisions?

970. Do friends perform better than acquaintances?

971. Which situations call for a more extreme type of adaptiveness in which team members actually re-define roles?

972. Can familiarity breed backup?

973. How hard do you try to make a good selection?

974. What are teams?

975. Is there a particular method of data analysis that you would recommend as a means of demonstrating that method variance is not of great concern for a given dataset?

976. When does the medium matter?

977. To what degree will the team ensure that all members equitably share the work essential to the success of the team?

978. To what degree can the team ensure that all members are individually and jointly accountable for the teams purpose, goals, approach, and work-products?

3.9 Team Member Performance Assessment: Red Hat OpenShift

979. Who should attend?

980. Verify business objectives. Are they appropriate, and well-articulated?

981. Are the goals SMART ?

982. What stakeholders must be involved in the development and oversight of the performance plan?

983. What were the challenges that resulted for training and assessment?

984. How do you currently use the time that is available?

985. What qualities does a successful Team leader possess?

986. What is a general description of the processes under performance measurement and assessment?

987. Should a ratee get a copy of all the raters documents about the employees performance?

988. What specific plans do you have for developing effective cross-platform assessments in a blended learning environment?

989. To what degree do team members feel that the

purpose of the team is important, if not exciting?

990. Is it clear how goals will be accomplished?

991. What are best practices for delivering and developing training evaluations to maximize the benefits of leveraging emerging technologies?

992. To what degree does the team possess adequate membership to achieve its ends?

993. For what period of time is a member rated?

994. To what degree do members articulate the goals beyond the team membership?

995. How do you start collaborating?

996. To what degree does the teams approach to its work allow for modification and improvement over time?

997. What entity leads the process, selects a potential restructuring option and develops the plan?

998. How should adaptive assessments be implemented?

3.10 Issue Log: Red Hat OpenShift

999. Is the issue log kept in a safe place?

1000. Persistence; will users learn a work around or will they be bothered every time?

1001. What is the stakeholders political influence?

1002. Who reported the issue?

1003. Who were proponents/opponents?

1004. How is this initiative related to other portfolios, programs, or Red Hat OpenShift projects?

1005. What is the impact on the risks?

1006. What is the status of the issue?

1007. How do you reply to this question; you am new here and managing this major program. How do you suggest you build your network?

1008. Are stakeholder roles recognized by your organization?

1009. Do you feel a register helps?

1010. Are the stakeholders getting the information they need, are they consulted, are concerns addressed?

1011. What does the stakeholder need from the team?

1012. Why multiple evaluators?

1013. What date was the issue resolved?

4.0 Monitoring and Controlling Process Group: Red Hat OpenShift

1014. Is there undesirable impact on staff or resources?

1015. How should needs be met?

1016. What resources are necessary?

1017. Is there sufficient funding available for this?

1018. Do the partners have sufficient financial capacity to keep up the benefits produced by the programme?

1019. Who needs to be engaged upfront to ensure use of results?

1020. Where is the Risk in the Red Hat OpenShift project?

1021. In what way has the program come up with innovative measures for problem-solving?

1022. Are there areas that need improvement?

1023. What resources (both financial and non-financial) are available/needed?

1024. Who are the Red Hat OpenShift project stakeholders?

1025. How is agile Red Hat OpenShift project management done?

1026. What departments are involved in its daily operation?

1027. What business situation is being addressed?

1028. What areas were overlooked on this Red Hat OpenShift project?

1029. How was the program set-up initiated?

1030. What factors are contributing to progress or delay in the achievement of products and results?

4.1 Project Performance Report: Red Hat OpenShift

1031. To what degree can the cognitive capacity of individuals accommodate the flow of information?

1032. To what degree do team members articulate the teams work approach?

1033. To what degree are the goals ambitious?

1034. To what degree does the informal organization make use of individual resources and meet individual needs?

1035. To what degree does the teams work approach provide opportunity for members to engage in open interaction?

1036. To what degree does the information network provide individuals with the information they require?

1037. To what degree do the goals specify concrete team work products?

1038. To what degree is there centralized control of information sharing?

1039. Next Steps?

1040. To what degree are fresh input and perspectives systematically caught and added (for example, through information and analysis, new members, and senior sponsors)?

1041. To what degree does the teams work approach provide opportunity for members to engage in results-based evaluation?

1042. To what degree does the task meet individual needs?

1043. To what degree is the team cognizant of small wins to be celebrated along the way?

1044. To what degree do team members agree with the goals, relative importance, and the ways in which achievement will be measured?

1045. To what degree does the teams purpose contain themes that are particularly meaningful and memorable?

1046. To what degree can team members frequently and easily communicate with one another?

4.2 Variance Analysis: Red Hat OpenShift

1047. Can the contractor substantiate work package and planning package budgets?

1048. Are there changes in the direct base to which overhead costs are allocated?

1049. Are overhead costs budgets established on a basis consistent with the anticipated direct business base?

1050. Contract line items and end items?

1051. Does the contractor use objective results, design reviews and tests to trace schedule performance?

1052. What are the direct labor dollars and/or hours?

1053. How do you identify and isolate causes of favorable and unfavorable cost and schedule variances?

1054. When, during the last four quarters, did a primary business event occur causing a fluctuation?

1055. How does the monthly budget compare to the actual experience?

1056. Who are responsible for overhead performance control of related costs?

1057. Are the requirements for all items of overhead established by rational, traceable processes?

1058. What causes selling price variance?

1059. Did an existing competitor change strategy?

1060. How are material, labor, and overhead variances calculated and recorded?

1061. Why do variances exist?

1062. Is the anticipated (firm and potential) business base Red Hat OpenShift projected in a rational, consistent manner?

1063. What can be the cause of an increase in costs?

4.3 Earned Value Status: Red Hat OpenShift

1064. Where is evidence-based earned value in your organization reported?

1065. Verification is a process of ensuring that the developed system satisfies the stakeholders agreements and specifications; Are you building the product right? What do you verify?

1066. How does this compare with other Red Hat OpenShift projects?

1067. How much is it going to cost by the finish?

1068. What is the unit of forecast value?

1069. When is it going to finish?

1070. Validation is a process of ensuring that the developed system will actually achieve the stakeholders desired outcomes; Are you building the right product? What do you validate?

1071. Are you hitting your Red Hat OpenShift projects targets?

1072. If earned value management (EVM) is so good in determining the true status of a Red Hat OpenShift project and Red Hat OpenShift project its completion, why is it that hardly any one uses it in information systems related Red Hat OpenShift projects?

1073. Earned value can be used in almost any Red Hat OpenShift project situation and in almost any Red Hat OpenShift project environment. it may be used on large Red Hat OpenShift projects, medium sized Red Hat OpenShift projects, tiny Red Hat OpenShift projects (in cut-down form), complex and simple Red Hat OpenShift projects and in any market sector. some people, of course, know all about earned value, they have used it for years - but perhaps not as effectively as they could have?

1074. Where are your problem areas?

4.4 Risk Audit: Red Hat OpenShift

1075. What is the implication of budget constraint on this process?

1076. Are end-users enthusiastically committed to the Red Hat OpenShift project and the system/product to be built?

1077. Number of users of the product?

1078. Assessing risk with analytical procedures: do systemsthinking tools help auditors focus on diagnostic patterns?

1079. What is happening in other jurisdictions? Could that happen here?

1080. How do you compare to other jurisdictions when managing the risk of ....?

1081. Can analytical tests provide evidence that is as strong as evidence from traditional substantive tests?

1082. Which assets are important?

1083. Do staff understand the extent of duty of care?

1084. Do you have a clear plan for the future that describes what you want to do and how you are going to do it?

1085. Does the implementation method matter?

1086. Are policies communicated to all affected?

1087. Do you have written and signed agreements/ contracts in place for each paid staff member?

1088. Do you have proper induction processes for all new paid staff and volunteers who have a specific role and responsibility?

1089. Who is responsible for what?

1090. Is all required equipment available?

1091. Is an annual audit required and conducted of your financial records?

1092. What are the strategic implications with clients when auditors focus audit resources based on business-level risks?

1093. Auditor independence: a burdensome constraint or a core value?

4.5 Contractor Status Report: Red Hat OpenShift

1094. What is the average response time for answering a support call?

1095. Are there contractual transfer concerns?

1096. Describe how often regular updates are made to the proposed solution. Are corresponding regular updates included in the standard maintenance plan?

1097. How is risk transferred?

1098. If applicable; describe your standard schedule for new software version releases. Are new software version releases included in the standard maintenance plan?

1099. What process manages the contracts?

1100. What was the actual budget or estimated cost for your organizations services?

1101. How does the proposed individual meet each requirement?

1102. What was the overall budget or estimated cost?

1103. What are the minimum and optimal bandwidth requirements for the proposed solution?

1104. How long have you been using the services?

1105. What was the budget or estimated cost for your organizations services?

1106. What was the final actual cost?

1107. Who can list a Red Hat OpenShift project as organization experience, your organization or a previous employee of your organization?

4.6 Formal Acceptance: Red Hat OpenShift

1108. Do you buy-in installation services?

1109. Have all comments been addressed?

1110. How well did the team follow the methodology?

1111. Was the Red Hat OpenShift project managed well?

1112. What are the requirements against which to test, Who will execute?

1113. Was the sponsor/customer satisfied?

1114. How does your team plan to obtain formal acceptance on your Red Hat OpenShift project?

1115. What features, practices, and processes proved to be strengths or weaknesses?

1116. Was the Red Hat OpenShift project goal achieved?

1117. Do you perform formal acceptance or burn-in tests?

1118. Is formal acceptance of the Red Hat OpenShift project product documented and distributed?

1119. Does it do what Red Hat OpenShift project team

said it would?

1120. What can you do better next time?

1121. Do you buy pre-configured systems or build your own configuration?

1122. Who supplies data?

1123. What lessons were learned about your Red Hat OpenShift project management methodology?

1124. General estimate of the costs and times to complete the Red Hat OpenShift project?

1125. What is the Acceptance Management Process?

1126. Was the client satisfied with the Red Hat OpenShift project results?

1127. What function(s) does it fill or meet?

5.0 Closing Process Group: Red Hat OpenShift

1128. What could be done to improve the process?

1129. What areas were overlooked on this Red Hat OpenShift project?

1130. Is the Red Hat OpenShift project funded?

1131. Does the close educate others to improve performance?

1132. What were the actual outcomes?

1133. What areas does the group agree are the biggest success on the Red Hat OpenShift project?

1134. What communication items need improvement?

1135. Is the Red Hat OpenShift project funded?

1136. Based on your Red Hat OpenShift project communication management plan, what worked well?

1137. What is the Red Hat OpenShift project name and date of completion?

1138. Who are the Red Hat OpenShift project stakeholders?

1139. Were cost budgets met?

1140. What could have been improved?

1141. Did the Red Hat OpenShift project team have the right skills?

1142. Was the schedule met?

5.1 Procurement Audit: Red Hat OpenShift

1143. Are there procedures for trade-in arrangements?

1144. Is there a policy on making purchases locally where possible?

1145. Are proper financing arrangements taken?

1146. Do procedures require cash advances to be returned by transferred or terminated employees before they can receive final paychecks?

1147. Proper and complete records of transactions and events are maintained?

1148. Are unusual uses of organization funds investigated?

1149. Are goods generally ordered and received in time to be used in the programs for which they were ordered?

1150. Are vendor price lists regularly updated?

1151. Are procurement policies and practices in line with (international) good practice standards?

1152. Are payment generated from computer programs reviewed by supervisory personnel prior to distribution?

1153. What is the process cost of the procurement function?

1154. Could bidders learn all relevant information straight from the tender documents?

1155. Were additional works brought about by a cause which had not previously existed?

1156. Are regulations and protective measures in place to avoid corruption?

1157. Is there no evidence of collusion between bidders?

1158. Are the responsibilities of the purchasing department clearly defined?

1159. Has management taken the necessary steps to ensure that relevant control systems are always up to date?

1160. Did the chosen procedure ensure fair competition and transparency?

1161. Are purchase orders pre-numbered?

1162. Were products/services not received within the prescribed time limit?

5.2 Contract Close-Out: Red Hat OpenShift

1163. Has each contract been audited to verify acceptance and delivery?

1164. Change in attitude or behavior?

1165. Was the contract type appropriate?

1166. Was the contract complete without requiring numerous changes and revisions?

1167. Have all contracts been completed?

1168. Have all contract records been included in the Red Hat OpenShift project archives?

1169. How/when used ?

1170. How does it work?

1171. Change in circumstances?

1172. Parties: who is involved?

1173. Are the signers the authorized officials?

1174. Why Outsource?

1175. Parties: Authorized?

1176. Change in knowledge?

1177. Have all contracts been closed?

1178. What happens to the recipient of services?

1179. How is the contracting office notified of the automatic contract close-out?

1180. What is capture management?

1181. Was the contract sufficiently clear so as not to result in numerous disputes and misunderstandings?

1182. Have all acceptance criteria been met prior to final payment to contractors?

5.3 Project or Phase Close-Out: Red Hat OpenShift

1183. Have business partners been involved extensively, and what data was required for them?

1184. What was learned?

1185. What is a Risk Management Process?

1186. Planned completion date?

1187. What process was planned for managing issues/ risks?

1188. What is a Risk?

1189. What was the preferred delivery mechanism?

1190. What was expected from each stakeholder?

1191. What are they?

1192. What advantages do the an individual interview have over a group meeting, and vice-versa?

1193. Did the delivered product meet the specified requirements and goals of the Red Hat OpenShift project?

1194. What information did each stakeholder need to contribute to the Red Hat OpenShift projects success?

1195. What went well?

1196. Who exerted influence that has positively affected or negatively impacted the Red Hat OpenShift project?

1197. What were the goals and objectives of the communications strategy for the Red Hat OpenShift project?

1198. Is there a clear cause and effect between the activity and the lesson learned?

1199. What is this stakeholder expecting?

1200. What are the marketing communication needs for each stakeholder?

5.4 Lessons Learned: Red Hat OpenShift

1201. Were all interests adequately involved/informed?

1202. How many interest groups are stakeholders?

1203. How much communication is task-related?

1204. Overall, how effective were the efforts to prepare you and your organization for the impact of the product/service of the Red Hat OpenShift project?

1205. Was Red Hat OpenShift project performance validated or challenged?

1206. Where could you improve?

1207. How mature are the observations?

1208. Were quality procedures built into the Red Hat OpenShift project?

1209. How well defined were the acceptance criteria for Red Hat OpenShift project deliverables?

1210. Was there enough support – guidance, clerical support, training?

1211. What is the supplier dependency?

1212. What solutions or recommendations can you

offer that would have improved some aspect of the Red Hat OpenShift project?

1213. Recommendation: what do you recommend should be done to ensure that others throughout your organization can benefit from what you have learned?

1214. What were the main bottlenecks on the process?

1215. How was the Red Hat OpenShift project controlled?

1216. How many government and contractor personnel are authorized for the Red Hat OpenShift project?

1217. What surprises did the team have to deal with?

1218. Did the Red Hat OpenShift project change significantly?

1219. Where do you go from here?

1220. How efficient were Red Hat OpenShift project team meetings conducted?

Index

control 2, 60, 65-69, 72-74, 136, 144-145, 150-151, 174, 179, 183, 193, 223, 244, 246, 279, 282, 294-297, 316-317, 322, 331-332, 353, 358, 361-362, 366, 382, 384, 397
controlled   72, 240, 294, 297, 403
controller   70, 73
controls   47, 67, 168, 203, 210, 259, 305
converged   86, 104
conversion   247, 291
convey   1
convince   193
cooperate   183, 322
Copyright   1
correct37, 65, 142, 178, 278, 315-316
correction   295
corrective   68, 142, 156, 203, 215, 280-281, 336, 342, 368
correctly   29
correspond   12-13
corruption   397
costing247, 294, 319
costumer   259
counselled   250
counting   161, 299
countries   92
couple 100, 137
course 31, 248, 387
covered   132, 269
covering   12
crashes   114
create 22, 112, 125, 151, 190, 223, 238, 311, 361
created   52, 106, 135, 138, 141-142, 159, 197, 201, 209, 272, 275, 277, 279, 311, 317, 358
creating   11, 79, 153, 288, 290
creativity   61
credible   183, 322
criteria 2, 5-6, 8, 12-13, 30, 56, 59, 130, 132, 140, 148, 151, 177, 184, 189, 213, 216, 261, 267-268, 280, 287-288, 312, 315, 321, 335, 349, 351-353, 399, 402
CRITERION   2, 19, 26, 37, 43, 54, 65, 75
critical 27, 30, 52, 73, 142-143, 161, 165, 173, 227-228, 237, 257, 263, 291, 303, 312, 350, 357, 366, 374
criticism   237
crossed   89
crucial 49, 136, 174, 357

privileged   103
probably   309
problem   19, 21-22, 26, 28, 30, 32-33, 50, 136, 146, 221, 223,
228, 245, 248, 359, 366, 387
problems   22-23, 63, 68, 242, 276, 330, 352
procedure   224, 235, 258, 260, 294, 368, 372, 397
procedures   13, 65, 69, 71, 143, 152-153, 157, 169, 173-174,
179, 181, 187-188, 191, 214, 217, 250, 281, 291, 294-295, 297, 307,
315, 317, 330, 350, 353, 366, 373, 388, 396, 402
proceeding   175, 177
process   1-6, 8-9, 11, 13, 27, 30-31, 34-35, 38-41, 44, 46-52,
55, 58, 62-63, 66, 69-74, 131, 138-139, 142, 144-145, 147-148, 150-
151, 153, 157, 159, 169, 174, 176, 191-192, 201, 205-208, 216, 219,
227, 229, 232-233, 242, 248-250, 252, 255-256, 264-266, 268, 275,
277-278, 280, 282-283, 285-286, 288-291, 307, 312, 314, 317, 325-
326, 329-330, 334, 342, 344-345, 349, 352-353, 357, 361, 370-371,
374, 377, 380, 386, 388, 390, 393-394, 397, 400, 403
processes   28, 46, 66, 139, 142, 150, 174, 191, 217, 225, 242-
243, 255-256, 281, 289, 297, 325, 329, 353, 357, 364, 369, 376,
385, 389, 392
processing   42
proclaim   31
procuring   143
produce   139, 169, 222, 256, 275, 307, 360
produced   242, 380
produces   163
producing   148, 286, 288
product   1, 87, 133, 151, 165, 174, 185-186, 190, 202, 208,
215, 222, 232, 248-250, 276, 282, 303, 324, 339-340, 345, 347, 359-
360, 363, 371, 386, 388, 392, 400, 402
production   41, 73, 75, 82, 86, 108, 110, 126, 132, 258
productive   62
products   1, 37, 51, 77, 114, 124, 137, 139, 148, 182, 206,
222, 226, 270, 286, 318, 343, 359, 363, 381-382, 397
profession   202, 340
profile 229, 367
profiling   50
profit 189
program   29, 87, 123, 139, 219, 250, 275-276, 340, 342, 378,
380-381
programme   242-243, 380
programs   221, 241, 250, 275, 359, 362, 378, 396

required   27-28, 34-35, 48, 56, 132, 137, 147, 153, 161, 163-164, 191, 193, 203, 205, 234, 242, 250, 259, 263, 274, 280, 285, 295, 300-301, 313, 328, 334-335, 355, 367, 389, 400
requires   214
requiring   135, 261, 272, 398
research   35, 93, 99, 230, 238, 265, 304, 367
resemble   357
reserved   1
reserves   159-160
reside 198, 352
resolution   150
resolve 164, 232
resolved   201, 211, 219, 243, 316, 319, 327, 379
resource   3-4, 7-8, 39, 67, 74, 83, 98, 106, 138, 144, 152, 157, 159, 164, 169, 171-172, 179, 197, 215, 221, 273, 307, 309, 335, 360
resourced   367
resources   2, 11, 22, 33, 60, 76, 88, 114, 123, 131, 136, 151, 161, 163, 168, 171-172, 174-175, 178-179, 183, 188, 211, 244-246, 271, 273-275, 280, 282, 295, 297, 300-301, 305, 313, 321, 324, 335, 349, 357, 380, 382, 389
respect   1
respond   111, 204, 276
responded   15
response   65, 68, 71, 73-74, 213, 252, 340, 356, 390
responses   55, 213-214, 342, 352
responsive   54, 183, 321
restart 95
restores   127
restrict 98
result   52, 57, 181, 184, 190, 225, 237, 262-263, 276, 322-323, 337, 363, 399
resulted   69, 376
resulting   43
results 12, 27, 35, 54, 62, 68, 132, 139, 142-143, 173, 178, 184, 189-191, 239, 243, 254, 256, 275-276, 278, 281, 301, 322, 327, 349, 357, 380-381, 384, 393
Retain 75
return 37, 191, 201, 329, 344
returned   396
review 13, 140, 177, 223, 229-230, 316, 326, 361, 366
reviewed   30, 150-151, 153, 203, 289, 327, 396
reviewers   237
reviews 124, 143, 150, 167, 198, 259, 290, 305, 325, 345, 349, 384